800 years of
FINNISH
ARCHITECTURE

800 years of FINNISH ARCHITECTURE

J M Richards

David & Charles
Newton Abbot . London . Vancouver

British Library Cataloguing in Publication Data

Richards, James Maude
  Eight hundred years of Finnish architecture.
  1. Architecture – Finland – History
  I. Title II. Guide to Finnish architecture
  720'.9471   NA1455.F5

  ISBN 0–7153–7512–1

© J. M. Richards 1978

Typeset by HBM Typesetting Limited, Chorley
and printed in Great Britain
by Biddles Limited, Guildford
for David & Charles (Publishers) Limited
Brunel House Newton Abbot Devon

Published in the United States of America
by David & Charles Inc
North Pomfret Vermont 05053 USA

Published in Canada
by Douglas David & Charles Limited
1875 Welch Street North Vancouver BC

Contents

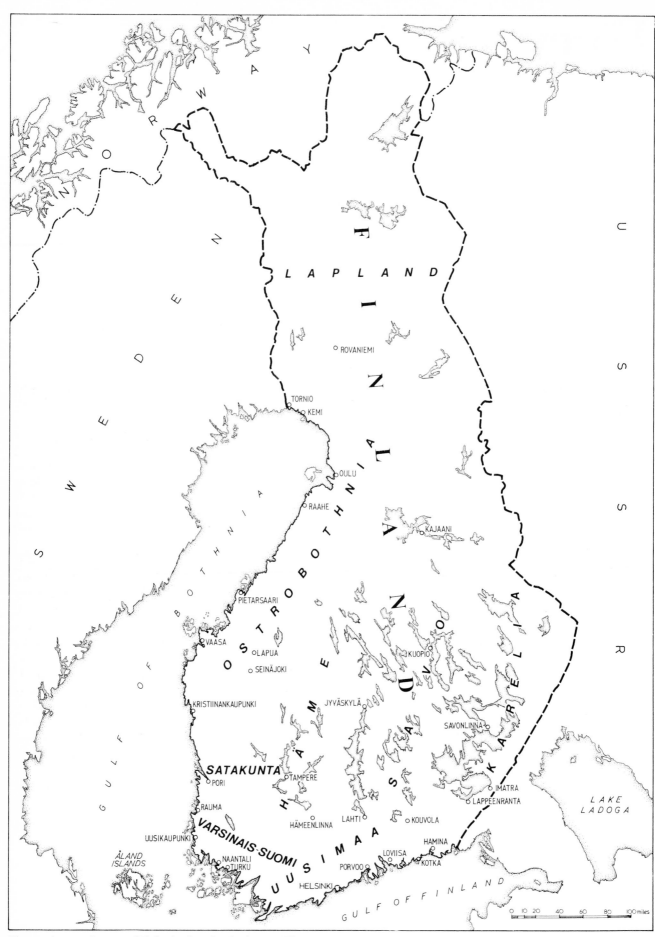

The provinces and towns of Finland referred to in the text. The
former are the old, traditional ones and are shown in bold lettering
to indicate their approximate areas. Boundaries are not marked
because no definitive version exists

Foreword

My *Guide to Finnish Architecture* was published in 1966 and has been out of print for some years. This book is intended to replace it and at the same time to improve on it, because the earlier book dealt only sketchily with several aspects of Finnish architecture which deserve more detailed treatment, and there were some gaps in it.

Therefore, although some of the text on the following pages repeats that in the earlier book, additions have been made to every chapter and some chapters have been rewritten, notably those on fortresses, on country houses, on the National Romantic Movement and on the wooden houses of which all Finnish towns were once composed and which are rapidly disappearing (although conservation measures have been initiated in the last two or three years). One altogether new chapter has been added—on rural vernacular buildings. The chapter on contemporary architecture has been brought up to date to include a number of important new buildings completed since 1966. In each chapter a new selection of pictures has been made, and the number of pictures, as well as the length of the text, is greater than in the earlier book.

The structure remains the same: an introductory essay on Finnish architecture and its special characteristics is followed by chapters on buildings of different types and periods, eg medieval churches, country houses, civic buildings of the eighteenth and nineteenth centuries and so on. But when the book reaches the end of the nineteenth century, each successive episode is treated as a whole without subdivision into building types, the main episodes being National Romanticism (together with the peculiarly Finnish version of *Art Nouveau*), the beginnings of modern architecture in the 1920s and 1930s and architecture after 1945.

Within each chapter the illustrations and the notes that accompany them are arranged as far as possible chronologically, except in the last chapter—on contemporary architecture—where they are arranged first of all according to their location, and then chronologically. Just over half the photographs were taken by myself. The sources of the others—mostly publishing houses and institutions in Finland, including especially the Museum of Finnish Architecture in Helsinki—are acknowledged on page 189.

I must thank the Finnish Ministry of Foreign Affairs and the Museum of Finnish Architecture for their invaluable help when I toured Finland in the summer of 1977 to collect the new material needed for this book. That was, I think, my ninth visit to Finland, which I first went to in 1934. I am especially indebted to Mr Aarno Ruusuvuori, the director of the museum, and to two members of the staff: Mr Asko Salokorpi and Mrs Raija-Liisa Heinonen. I should also like to renew my thanks to the previous director, the late Kyösti Ålander, for his help over the earlier book on which this one is based, and for his constructive criticism when it came out.

Finally, a note about place-names: many places in Finland have both a Finnish and a Swedish name. Throughout this book I have normally used the Finnish name, but I have given the Swedish name also when it differs substantially.

J.M.R.

1 Finland and its Architecture

Finland is better known for its modern than for its historic buildings, but that is only natural, because during the past forty years or more the Finnish contribution to the art of architecture has been far greater than that of many more populated countries. In the person of Alvar Aalto, Finland possessed one of the hero figures of modern architecture—one whose work had a warmth and naturalness that evoked a more immediate response in most people's eyes than the more didactic work of the other modern masters—and for many years Finland basked in the limelight his reputation brought to his country.

To those who knew Finland, however, it was clear that modern Finnish architecture was more than one man thick, and the final chapter of this book provides evidence of the distinguished work done by many other architects, and of the high standard this small country still maintains.

In recent years one other phase of Finnish architecture has deservedly been given attention. As part of a general growth of interest in the various *fin-de-siècle* developments such as *Art Nouveau*, the significance of the Finnish contribution to the revolutionary architectural movements of the end of the last century, expressed in the work of Lars Sonck, Eliel Saarinen and others, has now been fully recognized. But the Finnish architecture of earlier centuries has continued to be ignored, except by specialists. This, too, is natural since it has neither the seminal nor the spectacular qualities to be found in other European countries, Finland having been, for many of those centuries, only on the fringe of the civilized world. Moreover, because of the predominating use of timber, many early buildings have not survived. The history of most Finnish towns is a history of a succession of disastrous fires.

Yet the earlier Finnish architecture deserves to be noticed. It has a personality of its own and several episodes in its history—the building of village churches in the late medieval period and the achievements of Carl Ludwig Engel in the neoclassical style which transformed Helsinki, after about 1817, into the elegant city it still is, as well as the period of National Romanticism at the end of the nineteenth century—made a unique contribution to architectural history and can be studied today in buildings that are distinguished even by international standards.

The aim of this book is to bring accounts of early and of more recent Finnish architecture into the same perspective and to link the two together; a logical process because the influences that have shaped Finland herself—her history, her climate and topography and the temperament of her people—are the common thread on which the story of all her architecture must be strung.

For a long while, as I have just observed, Finland existed only on the fringe of civilization, and some of the characteristics of Finnish architecture derive from this: for example the absence of great monuments of the cathedral-building age (Christianity came late, and Finland was little influenced by Christian culture until long after the greatest era of medieval art; only the cathedral at Turku compares with the great Gothic structures that represented the power of the church in other European countries), and the corresponding circumstance that the use of an architectural style employing the language of the Renaissance became general only at the end of the eighteenth century when that style had almost run its course elsewhere in Europe and was there becoming either precious or debased.

Finland's history has, however, other characteristics from which the architecture that remains from her past derives more positive qualities. For example, unlike their Continental neighbours, the Finnish peasants were never serfs, and this is reflected in the self-sufficiency of the village communities which were not, as in feudal societies, dependent on great houses or castles. There are no vast country mansions; the more modest country houses—which exist in any case only in certain limited areas of the country—are small in scale and pretension and the castles, instead of being the residences of a landed aristocracy, are purely military fortresses.

In spite of her geographically remote situation, Finland did not escape European dynastic rivalries and struggles for power; on the contrary, Finland was one of the meeting grounds of the West and the East, and the changes and conflicts this position involved are written into her history and visible in her architecture. Victory was most often with the West—or often enough at least to ensure that Finland was dominated by Western culture, arriving mainly by way of Sweden, but to some extent from across the Baltic. Only parts of the Karelian provinces were subject, over the centuries, to strong Byzantine-Russian influences; Russian contacts with Finland generally were military rather than cultural. The obvious exception is the first few decades after 1809, when Finland became a grand duchy of the Russian Empire and the flow of political, and to a lesser extent cultural, influence was from the East to the West; but even then, since the point of origin was St Petersburg, and St Petersburg (Peter the Great's 'window on the West') was the most European of Russian cities, Helsinki, which was rebuilt at this time, remained in style a Western capital.

In one way only, perhaps, is a resemblance to Russia evident: in the layout of Finnish towns. They have much the same over-all character as the towns of northern Europe generally, except for the great breadth of the streets in relation to the height of the buildings. Similar space-giving proportions are of course found in Canada and the western United States where building in wood made it necessary, at the time the towns were first laid out, to take precautions against the spread of fire, and in all northern latitudes space has to be left on either side of the street for piling up the snow when the centre of the street is cleared; but a consistent townscape, determined by the proportions so caused, is typically Russian and, in this respect only, Finnish towns have a Russian aspect.

Finland's situation as a political—and for a large part of her history an actual—battleground has not only been responsible for the fragmentary nature of her architectural story over the centuries, but has coloured her architectural aspirations right up to modern times. Her energetic pursuit of a national style around 1900, and her ready adoption of modern architecture in the 1930s, can both be related to the Finns' self-awareness as a people able and anxious to control their own destinies, as well as reflecting the dour self-reliant qualities of a nation that has always had to fight for what it has achieved.

In addition there is the influence of climate and topography. The visitor to Finland—especially if he goes there in wintertime (most tourists go in the summer, when they make the acquaintance of the less typical, though perhaps more superficially agreeable, aspects of Finnish life)—is soon made aware of the hard unrelenting nature of the country, which its architecture clearly reflects. I do not mean that there is any absence of beauty in the ice-bound coastline, or in the forested landscape in which primeval rocks lie very near the surface, or the lakes in which the ripples caused by the wind are fixed and frozen for months at a time. These add up to a picture, coloured grey and white and muted shades of brown, that has its own special beauty; and so has the summertime picture, dominated by the green of forests and the changing blue and grey-blue of the endless waterways, and those who come to know the Finnish landscape develop a nostalgia for it that surprises them. But its beauty is of a kind that contains none of the exuberance, none of the sense of nature expending its superfluous energy, that we get in more southerly climates. In Finland nature and man must concentrate on holding their own.

This affects architecture in two ways: first it encourages a habit of persistent enquiry into technical possibilities—a search for new weapons with which to defeat and conquer the elements; and secondly, living so close to the more uncomfortable aspects of nature means that the essential relationship between the building, its materials and its setting is not easily lost sight of. This direct response to the forces of nature is the basis of the so-called organic quality that the great American architect Frank Lloyd Wright used to make so much of, and the work of Finland's outstanding modern architect, Alvar Aalto, exemplifies it strongly. Moreover, although the organic nature of the best Finnish architecture comes out so clearly in Aalto and those he has influenced (see Chapter 11 of this book, devoted to modern times) it is discernible also, along with a basic geometrical simplicity, in Finnish architecture of other periods.

But perhaps this is least apparent in Helsinki (Swedish, Helsingfors), where most visitors get their introduction to Finland, because Helsinki, though now a capital city with all the metropolitan qualities, is comparatively a young city. Before the Russians made it the capital in 1812, after capturing Finland from the Swedes, it was a small and unimportant town with a population of only 4,000. Then it was laid out afresh, according to a plan previously drawn up by Johan Albert Ehrenström after a disastrous fire had almost wholly destroyed it in 1808. The architectural embodiment of the new plan was the handsome sequence of squares and public buildings by Carl Ludwig Engel, described in Chapter 6.

They give a delightful consistency and formality to the centre of Helsinki, much as the Georgian squares and public buildings do to the centre of Dublin—another capital city to which Helsinki is in many ways comparable. Both Helsinki and Dublin possess the same seductive quality of light and the same clean-washed air that blows in from the sea, as well as the same arrangement of distinguished government and university buildings set among the architectural flotsam and jetsam of a commercial port, along with the broad perspectives that belong to a port that is at the same time the gateway to a country.

Another parallel could perhaps be drawn between Helsinki and Dublin by relating the cultural and social stresses set up by the domination of the English minority over the native Irish to those resulting from the domination of the Swedes and those who spoke Swedish, during much of Finland's history, over the less worldly-wise and sophisticated Finns, though this is not a parallel that need be stretched too far. Helsinki and Dublin are moreover much the same size. The population of greater Helsinki has not quite reached three-quarters of a million—an ideal size for a city of this kind; large enough to be fully metropolitan, but small and compact enough for its central area to be covered on foot.

The population of this and other Finnish towns are, however, inevitably increasing. At one time there seemed to be a firm policy of preventing growth from turning into sprawl by the use of planning devices designed to preserve the towns' shapeliness and comprehensibility. An outstanding example of such a device was Tapiola (Swedish, Hagalund), the dormitory town on the western fringe of Helsinki, which was so beautifully designed that it became internationally famous. It was built in the 1950s and early 1960s. Since then, unfortunately, similar means of controlling sprawl have not been adopted, and the two main residential areas west and northeast of the city, Espoo and Vantaa, which are administratively outside the city boundary, have been allowed to spread so widely and in so uncontrolled a fashion that today Espoo alone, with a population of 120,000, could contain the whole population of Finland if its density were no greater than that of Tapiola—itself well endowed with green spaces.

Other towns in Finland are spreading in the same way. The enlightened precedent of Tapiola has been followed up only in a few instances, such as the small satellite town of Hervanta (present population 12,000, but designed to grow to 40,000) on the southeastern edge of Tampere (which, though it indicates forethought iu planning, architecturally has nothing like the quality of Tapiola) and the far smaller satellite town of Lähderanta (Swedish, Källstrand) with a population of 3,000, designed by the architect Erik Kråkström and built between 1961 and 1966, 16km (10 miles) west of Helsinki.

Nevertheless, in spite of the untidy sprawl of its outlying residential areas, Helsinki remains a handsome capital. Being in effect only a century and a half old, it possesses no monuments of earlier date except the remains of the great eighteenth-century fortress of

Suomenlinna (Swedish, Sveaborg) on a cluster of islands in the harbour. Besides Engel's neoclassical buildings and a wide range of modern buildings of the last thirty years or so, the good buildings in which Helsinki is richest belong to the period of Romantic Nationalism that began soon after 1900 and is dealt with in Chapter 9. They were designed with remarkable conviction and a passionate belief in architecture's need to be rooted in local culture. Although this style, and the Finnish version of *Art Nouveau* which became to some extent mingled with it, was current for little more than a dozen years, while it lasted it dominated Finnish architecture in a way that occurred perhaps nowhere else. In other countries, although similar styles had their passing vogue and the *Art Nouveau* style in particular arose out of the same desire to escape from the straitjacket of academic historicism, they represented the work of a minority of eccentrics and devotees. The earnest search for a new architectural idiom on the part of nearly all the leading Finnish architects between 1900 and about 1912 gives a fresh and surprising flavour to parts of Helsinki and other Finnish cities—parts built up when London, for instance, was hardly looking beyond the most conventional Edwardian Baroque.

Before the rebuilding of Helsinki, the capital of Finland was Turku (Swedish, Åbo), and here isolated buildings do remain as evidence of the town's antiquity, notably the castle that commanded the sea approach to the town from a hill above the river Aura (the river that furnished the gateway through which European culture, and the Christianity that was its principal carrier, entered Finland) and the cathedral. The latter (see Chapter 3) is the one substantial building Finland possesses that can take its place among the Gothic cathedrals of Europe.

Around the cathedral, and between it and the river, is a charming group of neoclassical buildings dating mostly from the beginning of the nineteenth century (see Chapter 6), one of which was built for the first Åbo *Akademi*, the oldest university in Finland. Turku was replanned by the ubiquitous Engel after all but a small area near the cathedral had been destroyed by fire in 1827. His classical layout still survives, and this, and the river that runs through it, give Turku an agreeable sense of breadth and openness. It contains good examples of architecture of all periods in spite of the centre having been somewhat marred by commonplace rebuilding in recent years.

Tampere (Swedish, Tammerfors), Turku's rival as Finland's second largest, and leading industrial, city is more coherent and self-confident. Though founded in the eighteenth century, it is almost wholly modern in character and contains a number of distinguished recent buildings as well as a cathedral, finished in 1907, which is perhaps Lars Sonck's most important work. Towns, however, played a relatively small part in the early development of Finland, and in the other principal towns the architectural interest is likewise predominantly modern. In their visible form Finnish towns go back no further than a century and a half, though some were founded many years earlier—Pori (Swedish, Björneborg) in 1658; Vaasa in 1606; Oulu, in spite of being far to the north, in 1610; Kuopio in 1653. Porvoo (Swedish, Borgå), on the Gulf of Finland east of Helsinki, which received its charter as early as 1346, is exceptional in preserving an old quarter fairly intact. Here narrow streets of wooden houses lead up to its fifteenth-century church and an eighteenth-century town-hall, now a museum, fronts on to a sloping, cobbled square. Similar old quarters, reminders of the time when Finland was a flourishing centre of sea-going—indeed ocean-going—trade, survive in several of the towns along the western coast: Pietarsaari (Swedish, Jakobstad), Pori which I've already mentioned, Kristiinankaupunki (Swedish, Kristinestad) and Rauma in particular.

Here colonies of wooden houses surround the quays and waterfronts (from which in most cases the sea has now, in fact, receded so that the modern port installations have been built some miles to the west), and these towns are the places (see Chapter 7) in which to see the streets and squares of one- and two-storey wooden buildings of which Finnish towns were once wholly composed.

An unusual town is Hamina (Swedish, Fredrikshamn), still further east along the Gulf of Finland—in fact, since 1940, the last coastal town before the Russian frontier. It was rebuilt as a military centre in the eighteenth century, surrounded with fortifications, and has a symmetrical, radial street-plan forming a series of concentric octagons with the town-hall in the middle.

Other towns possess, perhaps, a neoclassical church or a nineteenth-century town-hall, and in some instances, for example, Loviisa and Hämeenlinna (Swedish, Tavastehus), the remnants of a formal layout as reminders that they go back at least to the time of the Russian Empire. But, for the reasons already given, their architecture is predominantly modern, though the principal towns—those already mentioned together with Lahti, Kotka, Rovaniemi, Jyväskylä, and others—have flourished long enough to have developed their own individuality. Vaasa, for example, has an unusually handsome sequence of squares and green spaces, having been laid out anew by the Swedish architect C. A. Setterberg after the town had been almost wholly destroyed by fire in 1852. Oulu (Swedish, Uleåborg) has recently completed the first stage (see pages 180-1) of an ambitious modern cultural and administrative centre, sited on the waterfront, which recalls the maritime importance the town has maintained since Hanseatic times; also the first stages of a new university some way outside the town (pages 180-1), recalling Oulu's long history as a centre of education.

Jyväskylä has a similar history, and its university is spaciously laid out in the very centre of the town, not far from where, in 1858, stood the first secondary school to provide teaching in the Finnish language. In Jyväskylä Alvar Aalto began his career. Both the university (pages 176-7) and the town museum are his work. Rovaniemi, the northernmost town of any size and the administrative capital of Finnish Lapland, is wholly modern and has not yet developed much character. Though established in the 1920s, it suffered in the same way as most of the older towns, being completely burnt by the retreating German army in 1944.

Most of these towns retain a few streets of wooden houses, eighty or ninety years old, of considerable charm with fretted gables and ornamented window-surrounds, although in larger towns the vernacular wooden architecture is inevitably disappearing.

If few Finnish towns possess buildings of much antiquity, in the villages, especially of western and southern Finland, medieval churches (see Chapter 3) are to be found in surprising numbers. About seventy of these survive, many with their original furnishings and wall-paintings. Other villages, especially in Ostrobothnia—the western coastal district—have neoclassical churches by Engel, or in the Engel style, built around 1820 or 1840. Whatever period they belong to, the village churches of Finland make a unique and too little known contribution to European architecture. They, together with the neoclassical buildings of Engel and his immediate predecessors, the vernacular wooden street architecture, the buildings associated with the romantic movement of the beginning of this century and the best of the buildings of the last thirty or forty years are those to which I have thought it right to give most attention.

One of the many medieval village churches in its typically Finnish setting; the early fifteenth-century church at Isokyrö in Ostrobothnia (see also page 32)

2 Fortresses

I use the term fortresses rather than castles to indicate that in Finland the purpose of the buildings described in this chapter was almost wholly military, whereas in most other countries castles filled, in addition, the social role of residences of the nobility. The only exception among all the Finnish castles was that at Turku, which, from the fourteenth century onwards, was the seat of the ducal court, and afterwards of the governor-general, but even in this case the purpose was administrative; the castle was never a family stronghold.

Finland is strewn with fortifications of a kind, having been so continually a battleground. The wars between the Swedes and the Russians, which were fought backwards and forwards across the Finnish countryside from the late sixteenth century until the early nineteenth, left behind great numbers of these, especially in the south-eastern region around Loviisa, Kotka and Lappeenranta where the new frontier was fixed in 1721 after Finland (still then under Swedish rule) had been compelled—not for the last time—to cede to Russia parts of Karelia and the town of Viipuri.

But these fortifications and the others like them survive as little more than systems of trenches and embankments and lengths of stone revetment buried in the woods. There are also fragmentary remains of far earlier castles; for example the fortifications of Linnanmäki (Swedish, Borgbacken) hill, at Porvoo, thought to be connected with a Danish expedition to Finland in about the year 1200, Vanhalinna Castle, at Lieto near Turku, built by the Swedes towards the end of the twelfth century on the site of an iron-age hill-fort, and Hakoinen Castle at Janakkala in Häme, connected with Birger Jarl's expedition to Finland in the middle of the thirteenth century. The last was abandoned when Hämeenlinna (see page 13) was built late in the same century.

Hämeenlinna was one of three large fortresses constructed at this time. The other two were Turun linna, the castle that stands above the estuary of the Aura river at Turku, and that of Viipuri, now in Soviet Russia. Two more were built in the fourteenth century: Raasepori on the coast of western Uusimaa, and Kastelholm in the Åland Islands. In the fifteenth century was built the most romantically situated castle in Scandinavia and one of the best preserved: Olavinlinna, outside the town of Savonlinna in eastern Finland.

Finland thus has five medieval fortresses surviving as substantial works of architecture, all described below: at Turku, Hämeenlinna, Raasepori, Kastelholm and Savonlinna. These were all royal castles. In addition, the bishops of Turku built several fortified residences, of which the most important was on Kuusisto Island in the archipelago. This was built in the fourteenth century but destroyed by King Gustav Vasa during the Reformation. A few ruined walls survive. Traces of the other bishops' castles are even less.

In 1604 King Carl IX of Sweden built a strong fortress at Kajaani in the remote northern country to defend the new settlements round Lake Oulujärvi, but this too was destroyed a hundred years later. In the eighteenth century fortifications were built round the town of Hamina (see page 72) and two island fortresses were constructed, also on Finland's south coast—Svartholm, protecting the Bay of Loviisa, and Suomenlinna, guarding the sea approaches to Helsinki. Little remains at Svartholm as a result of a British naval bombardment during the Crimean War, but Suomenlinna is a fascinating place; the visitor to Helsinki will find the fifteen-minute motor-boat trip from the South Harbour well worthwhile. This fortress, too, is described on page 17.

Turku (Swedish, Åbo)

Founded in the 1280s, the castle at Turku (Turun linna) stands on high ground commanding the harbour and the mouth of the river. It is visible from far out to sea. It originally consisted of two parallel four-storey buildings, separated at either end—east and west—by six-storey towers, all in grey stone. The castle was improved in the fourteenth century, when the vaulted King's Hall was built into the top storey of the north wing and the Nun's Chapel, with the earliest star-vaulting in Finland, in the east tower. In the fifteenth century two storeys were added to this tower. In the sixteenth century, when John, one of the sons of the Swedish king, Gustavus Vasa, became Duke of Finland, the residential part of the castle was further improved to house his court and an outer bailey was built on the slope of the hill.

The castle was afterwards held by Klaus Fleming, the governor who rebelled against the duke-regent, the future Charles IX. Charles

Turku. The castle (thirteenth to sixteenth century)

Hämeenlinna. The castle (thirteenth to sixteenth century) (see also page 14)

laid seige to it and captured it in 1599. In 1614, during a visit by Gustavus Adolphus, it was badly damaged by fire. After that it lost its military importance, though the habitable parts remained the residence of successive Swedish governors-general of Finland. These included the philanthropic Per Brahe who founded the Åbo *Akademi* (still the Swedish-language university) in 1640. By the eighteenth century, however, the castle had become so dilapidated that it was used only as a prison. Since 1881 it has been a museum. In 1941 its timber roofs were destroyed by bombing, but between 1944 and 1961 it was thoroughly restored.

Hämeenlinna (Swedish, Tavastehus)

The medieval castle of Häme is of the square type favoured by the Teutonic knights and is built mostly of brick—unusual in Finland. It was begun in the thirteenth century by Birger Jarl, and consisted then of a brick residential keep, with vaulted roofs, enclosed within stone walls with corner towers. In the fourteenth century a flanking tower was built. Later an encircling wall was also added and, in the sixteenth century, two stone rondels (foreground of photograph). In 1836 the castle became a prison, until 1953 when restoration work was started. It can be visited during the summer months only.

The castle of Hämeenlinna, from an engraving of 1710

Raasepori castle (thirteenth century)

Raasepori (Swedish, Raseborg)

Built in the late thirteenth century for coastal defence, the castle (near Tammisaari (Swedish, Ekenäs) in south-western Finland) is now a little way from the sea. It had a keep and an encircling wall, like Hämeenlinna on the Teutonic pattern. The Swedish king, Karl Knutson Bonde, held his court there in the 1460s. The castle was abandoned during the reign of Gustavus Vasa and became a ruin. Conservation work on the walls and their circular corner towers began at the end of last century.

Kastelholm

This is a late fourteenth-century castle in the Åland Islands, first occupied by the justiciar, Bo Jonsson Grip. It had a rectangular stone keep with a residential wing and was surrounded by a wall. A bailey was added on the north side in the fifteenth century and another on the east side in the sixteenth. Gustavus Vasa was a frequent visitor to Kastelholm. His son, Eric XIV, was imprisoned there and Gustavus Adolphus spent his honeymoon there. The castle was burnt by the Danes in 1507. It was repaired, but declined in importance during the seventeenth century and fell into decay. The north wing has lately been restored and houses the Åland provincial museum.

Kastelholm castle (fourteenth century)

**Savonlinna. The island castle of
Olavinlinna (fifteenth to
eighteenth century)**

Plan of Olavinlinna

1 Inner courtyard
2 Later courtyard
3 Suvarov's outer bastions
4 Bell tower
5 Chapel tower
6 South-east bastion
7 Knight's Hall

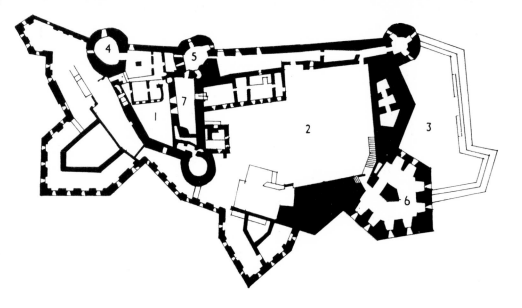

Suomenlinna (eighteenth century): King's Gate

Savonlinna

The castle of Olavinlinna is named after St Olof, patron saint of the Danish-born governor of Viipuri, Erik Axelsson Tott, who founded it in 1475. It occupies a rocky island in the southernmost of the two lakes between which the town of Savonlinna, in eastern Finland, is set. It was intended, together with the town walls of Viipuri, as a base for hostilities against Grand Duke Ivan III of Muscovy. After 1617 Finland's frontier was moved further east—too far for the castle to play an important military role. In 1714 and again in 1740 it fell into Russian hands.

The original castle had three circular corner towers, of which two survive, linked by ramparts enclosing a triangular stone-paved courtyard. Overlooking the courtyard was the rectangular Knight's Hall with living quarters beneath, and on the second floor of one of the towers was a stone-vaulted chapel. It also had an outer bailey. In the sixteenth century the castle was extended to the east to enclose a second, larger, courtyard whose walls were protected by a tower at the south-east corner of the island, built in 1562. This was destroyed in 1788 by the explosion of a powder-magazine and replaced by an angular bastion. Early in the seventeenth century another tower was built at the north-east corner, similar in style to the two original towers; this makes the third of the three circular towers prominent in the view of the castle from the shore of the lake. Their conical roofs date only from the eighteenth century.

After capturing the castle in 1740 the Russian General Suvarov added three bastions on the south side and extended them to the east. By the nineteenth century, following the complete conquest of Finland by Russia during the Napoleonic wars, Olavinlinna had lost its military usefulness. It became a prison and then, in the 1860s,

was abandoned and began to decay. Restoration work began in the 1870s. A second thorough restoration was completed in 1975. It is open in the summer.

Suomenlinna (Swedish, Sveaborg)

This powerful system of fortifications, occupying a cluster of islands in the harbour of Helsinki and designed to protect its seaward approaches, was begun in 1747. The work was directed by Augustin Ehrensvärd until his death in 1772. It was planned as both a naval and a military base and included a shipyard. Because of its reputed invincibility it was known as the Gibraltar of the North. Nevertheless it surrendered to the Russians in 1808 without firing a shot, but proved its strength later by withstanding the attack, during the Crimean War, of a joint British and French naval force. This bombardment (1855), however, destroyed the main headquarters buildings—a palatial governor's residence, officers' quarters, guardhouse etc—arranged in classical style round a courtyard.

Little is left of the other buildings, and the fortress now consists of a richly romantic landscape of grass-grown mounds and bastions and stone-faced gun emplacements spread over several islands. It is entered, by way of a small landing-stage, through the elliptical-arched King's Gate, on the flanking walls of which are inscribed tablets commemorating the founding of the fortress. One of the inner bastions has had a summer restaurant installed within it (architect, Aulis Blomstedt). There are also a garrison church, a naval museum and Ehrensvärd's tomb—the last designed by Gustavus III himself, together with J. T. Sergel. Suomenlinna can be visited throughout the year, even when most of Helsinki harbour is frozen over.

3 Medieval Churches

Christianity may be said to have established itself in Finland about 1229 when the first bishopric—later transferred to Turku and for centuries administering the whole country—was founded, though there had been earlier contacts with the Christian West. The Åland Islands, which now belong to Finland, had been Christianized and possessed stone churches with vaulted roofs as early as the beginning of the thirteenth century. The mainland was at this time a thinly populated—and indeed barely explored—wilderness, but following the so-called Crusades against Finland, organized by the Swedes from the mid-twelfth century onwards by order of the Pope, Christianity spread up the river-valleys of the south west and across the Häme region to Karelia. So energetically did Western culture penetrate the forests in its wake that, by the end of the thirteenth century, a number of the stone churches, that today so splendidly enrich the Finnish rural scene, had already been built, and many more, greatly influenced at first by Swedish models, were built during the fourteenth century. From that century also dates the cathedral at Turku.

The earliest village churches naturally arose in the extreme south west, the region around Turku. Among them was Nousiainen, where a bishop—the English-born Henry of Uppsala—had his seat even before the foundation of the bishopric of Turku. As stone-built churches spread to other parts of Finland, the different regions evolved their own characteristics. In the Åland Islands, for example, there was usually a western tower showing the influence of Gotland, an influence also to be found in Uusimaa, the southern region facing the Gulf of Finland, where there were many Swedish settlers. In Ostrobothnia, the flattish region bordering the Gulf of Bothnia, there were wooden churches, likewise showing Swedish influences, but all Finland's medieval wooden churches have now disappeared. Typical of many parts of the south and west are gables faced with patterned brickwork, derived originally, it is thought, from north German and Danish sources.

The Finnish stone-built village churches are nevertheless characteristically themselves, with a strength and simplicity befitting their role of frontier posts of Western Christianity. The typical church is a plain rectangle in plan, with aisles but without the narrower choir of earlier date, and without a tower. The walls are of undressed grey granite boulders. The nave is wider than the aisles, but no higher. At the beginning there was often wooden barrel-vaulting, but stone-vaulted sacristies were added quite early, and in the fourteenth century brick (or sometimes stone) cross-vaulting became general over the whole church, followed in the fifteenth century by star-vaulting over certain areas such as the central nave. The development of vaulting was influenced by the work going forward in Turku Cathedral throughout the fourteenth century.

These village churches are dominated externally by the great expanse of their shingle-covered roofs. There are usually two projections on the north and south sides: a sacristy and an armoury, the latter forming part of a south porch (see the plan of Hattula, page 28). There is an entrance in the centre of the west front, but not usually a window above it. The east end has a large window; the aisle windows are small but have in many cases been subsequently enlarged.

The brick decoration of the gables varies regionally; it may consist of groups of niches (said to symbolize, by their number, the Trinity, the twelve apostles and so on), perhaps a main niche in the form of a cross, or niches and recessed panels in arrangements of vertical stripes, bands and circles. The recessed parts of the design are picked out with whitewash; in the past they may have been coloured. These decorated gables achieved their greatest elaboration at the end of the fifteenth century and the beginning of the sixteenth, when some churches had new gabled fronts added. Apart from the gables, the use of brick was limited to door and window surrounds, internal pillars and vaulting. The church at Hattula is a rare example of a fourteenth-century country church built almost wholly of brick.

A number of these churches—Kumlinge, Inkoo, Hattula and Lohja are among the best examples—contain frescoes in a very good state of preservation, some as early as the end of the fourteenth century, and in several churches in the Åland Islands, the end of the thirteenth. They were painted with a dry technique (as distinct from the familiar Italian technique in which the paint is applied to still-wet plaster), and in some cases—Lohja, for example, where the frescoes are early sixteenth-century—the whole of the wall-surfaces, to-

Jomala church (twelfth to thirteenth century)

Jomala

gether with the piers and the vaulting, are covered with an enchantingly fresh and flowing design of figures and foliage. In many churches the ribs of the vaulting are striped and patterned in terracotta red.

Many village churches also contain good examples of wood sculpture. The best of this is from the sixteenth century and is thought to be the work of an itinerant German school of craftsmen, based in Stockholm.

A characteristic feature of nearly all Finnish churches, except those in the Åland Islands, is the free-standing bell-tower, which is usually, however, of a later date than the church itself, having in the first place been built of wood rather than stone and perhaps been several times replaced. Many bell-towers were rebuilt, again in wood, during the Engel (Russian Empire) period in a simple neoclassical style. Painted pale yellow or pale grey and white, they consort very happily with the grey stone, brick-gabled churches near which they stand in their tree-shaded graveyards, behind a foreground of granite tombstones, long grass and plant-tufted drystone boundary walls.

The following notes and accompanying illustrations describe some outstanding and typical examples of the seventy or so medieval churches that survive.

Among the earliest of Finland's medieval churches are those on the Åland Islands, and the village church at Jomala (9km, 5 miles north of Mariehamn, the chief town of the islands) contains work earlier than any other—in fact it is one of the oldest stone churches in Scandinavia. It is dedicated to St Olaf, patron saint of the islands, who is said to have converted their inhabitants to Christianity in the eleventh century. The church was built early in the twelfth century from which time the west wall and the tower survive in their original form. The remainder is thirteenth-century and follows the style of most Gotland churches, but the nave was enlarged and given a cruciform shape in the nineteenth century. At the same time the cupola was added to the tower. Fourteenth-century paintings—among the oldest in Finland—once decorated the whole interior, but only those on the west wall and the tower-arch survive. They were restored in 1932.

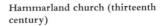
Hammarland church (thirteenth
century)

Lemland church (thirteenth
century)

Hammarland

This Åland Island village is 21km (13 miles) north west of Mariehamn. The church is thirteenth-century and is unusual in having a
chancel rather narrower than the nave and a tower placed at the
south-west corner. Both chancel and tower are a little later than the
nave. The interior has stone vaulting, probably not constructed until
the fifteenth century, and paintings—mostly floral scroll-work—of
the same date.

Lemland

Another thirteenth-century Åland Island church, this lies 12km (8
miles) south east of Mariehamn. The rectangular chancel has a
wooden ceiling and the remains of wall-paintings (dating from between 1280 and 1310) discovered only in 1956 when the church was
being restored. The archway separating the small square chancel
from the nave was once much narrower.

Finström church (late thirteenth
century; tower fifteenth century)

Finström

This large church of the late thirteenth century, built on the site of
an earlier wooden one, is about 24km (15 miles) north of Mariehamn. It is rectangular in plan with a small square chancel and a
heavy stone-ribbed barrel-vault supported by abutments pierced
with arches. The tower is fifteenth-century. Its shingle-covered
spire and corner pinnacles resemble those of many Swedish churches
of this time as well as those of some in Ostrobothnia (compare the
later wooden churches in that region shown in the next chapter).
The interior of Finström has several layers of wall-paintings and
some framed paintings of the apostles dating from the beginning of
the fifteenth century.

Kumlinge church (fifteenth century; spire, by Antti Piimänen, eighteenth century)

Nousiainen church (late thirteenth century)

Kumlinge

This is the last of the five Åland Island churches illustrated here, and also the smallest. It is on one of the outlying islands of the group—east of the main island and quite close to the Turku archipelago. The church was built in the fifteenth century and is unusual in having its bell-tower over the armoury which projects from its north side. This tower has a baroque spire, added in 1767 by Antti Piimänen. The interior has a vaulted roof and exceptionally fine, early sixteenth-century wall-paintings.

Nousiainen

This is one of the earliest stone village churches on the Finnish mainland, being situated north of Turku (about 24km, 15 miles), in the area where Christianity was first introduced. Nousiainen was in fact the seat of the first bishop, the English-born Henry of Uppsala, who was established there at the end of the twelfth century. The bishopric was transferred to Turku when the cathedral there was completed.

The present Nousiainen church, replacing an earlier wooden one, was built in Bishop Henry's memory in 1286–90. It has two chancels, one (projecting southwards) added later. The nave was redesigned in the late fourteenth century, with aisles. The piers are of brick. There are primitive wall-decorations, restored in 1936, a seventeenth-century pulpit and some good wood sculpture. The interior has been further restored recently, with new pews. Like many of the medieval churches on the Finnish mainland, Nousiainen has a detached wooden bell-tower of the early nineteenth century.

Turku (Swedish, Åbo)

The cathedral at Turku is the only major Gothic cathedral in Finland, although some smaller medieval churches (for example, that at Porvoo), being the seats of bishops, have the title of cathedral. The two other principal cathedrals, although architecturally im-

25

Turku cathedral: south side

Turku cathedral: interior looking east

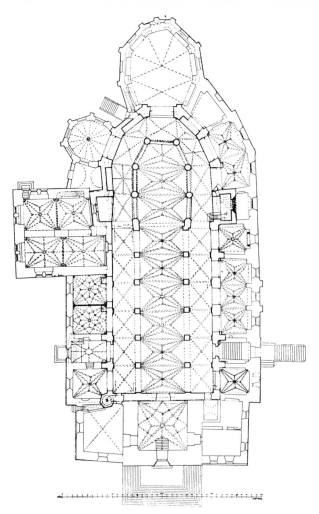

Plan of Turku cathedral

portant, are of much later date: that at Helskinki (by Engel, 1830–40) and that at Tampere (by Sonck, 1902–07). (These are described in Chapters 6 and 9.)

Turku Cathedral is beautifully sited, just across the river from the modern part of the town, on a grassy mound with elegant neo-classical buildings of the beginning of last century grouped around it. Their pale, smooth stucco walls serve as a foil to the cathedral's dark-red, pitted and textured brick, and the whole random complex of buildings is set among tall trees.

The cathedral was first built in 1286–92, but was largely destroyed by the Russians in 1318. It was then rebuilt and enlarged in a style influenced by the churches of the Teutonic Knights on the other side of the Baltic. It was at this time (early fourteenth century) that

the massive square western tower was built, to which corner turrets were added in mid-century; of the latter only traces remain. There was also a spire, later replaced by a curvilinear roof. This was destroyed by fire in 1827 and the present neo-Gothic central turret was built in its place, bringing the total height of the tower to 91m (300ft).

The cathedral began as an aisled hall-church, but in the fifteenth century chapels were added along either side and eventually combined to form, in effect, outer aisles (see plan). The side walls were subsequently raised and given clerestory windows, and new vaulting was built. In the middle of the fourteenth century a choir was added with octagonal pillars—those in the nave are square—and in the late fifteenth century an octagonal chapel was added at the east end. Also in the fifteenth century, the thirteenth-century sacristy at the northeast corner of the original church was enlarged and given a starvaulted roof.

The length of the building today is 87m (286ft) and the width 38m (127ft). The side chapels contain a number of good monuments, mostly of the seventeenth century. The Tavast Chapel (containing the remains of Magnus Tavast, a famous Catholic bishop of Turku who died in 1452) has a wrought-iron grille commissioned in 1425 by the bishop himself. Another famous bishop of Turku was Mikael Agricola (1508–57) who led Finland to adopt the Reformed (Lutheran) Church and who first translated the Bible into Finnish.

Inkoo

This church, in a village on the south coast, west of Helsinki, when first built in the thirteenth century was one of the earliest stone examples. It was enlarged in the fourteenth century and again at the end of the fifteenth—a period of very active church-building in the province of Uusimaa. Inside it has vaulting (forming a double nave) similar to that at Hollola, and medieval wall-paintings. The gable has a striking brick pattern employing a triple cross and groups of recessed rectangles and circles. The church shares a leafy rustic setting with a bell-tower of unusual form, consisting of a broad stone base and a three-tier wooden superstructure (eighteenth-century), each tier having a shingled roof.

Hattula

This is a rare instance of a medieval church built mostly in brick. Being only a few kilometres north of Hämeenlinna, it may have been influenced by the brick construction of Hämeenlinna Castle (see Chapter 2) which dates from about the same time—the early fourteenth century. Hattula Church stands among fields in a walled enclosure entered on the north and south sides through brick and stone gateways that repeat, on a smaller scale, the geometrical form of the church. On the west side is a bell-tower with a stone base and a nineteenth-century wooden superstructure.

The plan of the church, shown overleaf, is that of most Finnish medieval churches: an aisled rectangular nave with a sacristy pro-

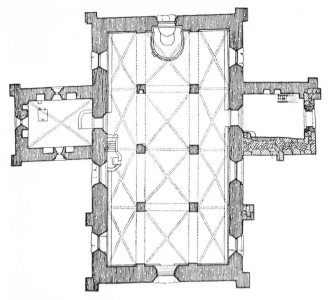

Plan of Hattula church

Tyrvää

This is a small, late fourteenth-century village church of the usual hall type. It stands at the end of a peninsula projecting into a lake some kilometres to the west of Tampere and thus on the borders of Satakunta. The building, which has been out of use as a church since 1855, is notable for the unusual form of the brick decoration on the gables which date from 1513–15. The east gable has a cross, with circular ends subdivided into stars, surmounted by an arch of niches, and the west gable a stepped rectangular decoration enclosing a round-headed central niche. Inside there is wooden barrel-vaulting possibly of the eighteenth century. The shingle roof, with its complex patterning, is an eighteenth-century replacement.

Rymättylä

This is a single-aisled fourteenth-century church with fifteenth-century star vaulting similar to that at Hollala. The village of Rymättylä is in the archipelago south west of Turku. The walls of the church and the vaulting are covered with richly foliated paintings, done about 1520, showing Renaissance influence.

Hattula church: interior with sixteenth-century paintings

Tyrvää church (fourteenth to sixteenth century)

jecting to the north and an armoury to the south. Hattula also has the typical very steeply pitched roof. The walls are 1.5m (5ft) thick, of a double skin of brick, filled with earth. The west gable has a primitive version of the brick patterning developed more elaborately in later churches. It takes the form of a recessed cross flanked by niches. Apart from this decoration on the gables, external embellishment is rare in the Finnish medieval churches, but Hattula has six sculptured masks set high up in the wall. The interior has cross-vaulting and the vaults, the walls and the plain square piers are covered with early sixteenth-century paintings, primitive in style but unusually delicate in colour. The church also has some good sculptured figures in wood.

Porvoo (Swedish, Borgå)

The cathedral (for Porvoo is the seat of a bishop) stands on high ground in the centre of the old part of the town, shown in the photograph from across the river. It has the usual detached bell-tower, crowned by a two-tier curvilinear roof added in the eighteenth century. The church itself was built in 1414–18, but its sanctuary was widened and the vaulting added about half a century later. The centre of the nave has the star-vaulting that was coming into general use about this time. The east gable is filled by an elaborate brick decoration attributed to Carsten Nübuhr. The stone walls are otherwise limewashed, as is customary in this province of Uusimaa.

Rymättylä church: interior with
sixteenth-century paintings

Porvoo cathedral (fifteenth
century): bell-tower on right with
eighteenth-century cupola

Lohja church: wall paintings
(1514-22)

Lohja church (early fifteenth
century)

Lohja

This town, about 72km (45 miles) west of Helsinki, has the largest
of the medieval stone churches. It was built early in the fifteenth
century and vaulted in the usual Uusimaa style later in the same
century. Lohja is also remarkable for the paintings that cover the
whole interior—walls, pillars and vaulting. They were done between
1514 and 1522. The church was restored in 1820 when the vicar
made plans for drastically altering it and removing the paintings. His
alterations were prevented, but the paintings were whitewashed
over soon afterwards and not re-exposed until 1952 when they were
found in good condition. They are a mixture of arabesques and
groups of figures, lively and expressive and of beautiful colour.

Parts of the church are fourteenth-century, but the nave and

vaulting are fifteenth. It has the usual triple-aisled hall plan and is nearly 18m (60ft) high. The gable has brick decoration of comparatively simple design. The projected 1820 remodelling included a new bell-tower as the existing one was in bad condition, and a design was made by Engel (the drawings still exist). The parish, however, decided that the cost was too great, and restored the old one with a very simple wooden superstructure. In recent years, unfortunately, the parish—Lohja having become a growing and prosperous industrial centre—has carried out so thorough a restoration, refurnishing the whole interior with shiny new wood, that, although the old paintings remain, the church has altogether lost the atmosphere and the feeling of antiquity it lately possessed.

Isokyrö

This is one of the more northerly of the medieval stone churches, in fact the only stone village church in Ostrobothnia. It stands on the Kyrönjoki river between Lapua and Vaasa where, in 1714, Finnish troops, in bitterly cold weather, lost a decisive battle against the Russians. The early fifteenth-century church, which has been out of use since 1878, has gables of wood boarding, which replaced the original stone gables in 1820. Inside there are wall-paintings done in 1560 and thought, on the evidence of their style, to be by a north German artist. They were covered over in the seventeenth century, but resorted in 1720 when the church was repaired, its wood vaulting renewed and its windows enlarged.

(*top left*)
Isokyrö church (early fifteenth century)

(*top right*)
Ulvila church (fifteenth century)

(*bottom left*)
Ulvila church: bell-tower

(*bottom right*)
Ulvila church: interior

Pyhtää church (fifteenth century)

Ulvila

This fifteenth-century church, a replacement of a church built as early as 1332, serves a village to the east of Pori and marks the original site of that town. It is notable for its vaulted interior, the plastered surface of which, and of the piers supporting the vault, is deeply if crudely scooped to produce a vigorously sculptural effect. The vaulting dates from the end of the fifteenth century. The church has a detached wooden bell-tower with an octagonal turret crowned by a spire.

Pyhtää

Another grey stone village church, between Loviisa and Kotka, in the late medieval style typical of Uusimaa. It was built in the mid-fifteenth century and was clearly influenced by the church at Porvoo. It has the usual rectangular plan with two aisles and star-vaulting over the nave. The vaulting rests on cruciform columns—a shape only found here, at Pernaja and at Sipoo (which is between Helsinki and Porvoo). Pyhtää Church retains its original brick-framed windows. Restoration in 1951 revealed wall-paintings of saints under the plaster, in a primitive style unique in Finland. Again the church has an unusual bell-tower, in this case with a square lower storey of whitewashed stone with a curved roof supporting an elegant, octagonal wooden cupola.

33

Hollola church (late fifteenth century)

Hollola

Standing high up above a rolling, well farmed countryside, in a thickly planted graveyard which was once enclosed by a defensive wall, the church at Hollola, not far from Lahti, is one of the best preserved and embellished of the later medieval village churches. Its walls of uncoursed stone have a beautiful texture and subtly varied colour. It has the usual brick decorated gables, and on the axis of the south porch stands a tall bell-tower, reputedly designed by Carl Ludwig Engel, although not built until 1848, eight years after his death. The bell-tower is so placed that the approach to the church is through the stone archway that forms its lower storey. Its upper storeys are of wood, painted pale yellow and white, and it terminates in a cylindrical domed cupola.

The church itself was built in 1480. It has a double-aisled plan with square brick piers carrying star-vaulting. The large armoury, in its usual position on the south side, is also vaulted. There is some good medieval ironwork—for example the door from the armoury into the church—and good figure-sculptures in wood.

Hollola church; bell-tower (1848)
by C. L. Engel

Siuntio church (fifteenth century; bell-tower on right, early nineteenth century)

Naantali church (fifteenth century; cupola by C. F. Adelcrantz, eighteenth century)

Siuntio

This small village, not far from Lohja, has a modest specimen of the typical fifteenth-century, grey stone church with round-headed windows inserted later, as was often done. Near the west end, but at an angle to it, stands a bell-tower with an early nineteenth-century wooden superstructure, painted grey and white, of a strange pagoda-like shape.

Naantali (Swedish, Nådendal)

Naantali is a small coastal town a short way west of Turku for which it serves as a summer resort. Its streets of decorated timber houses survive fairly intact (page 102). The town grew up round a monastery, founded in 1443 and suppressed during the Reformation, in which the earliest known Finnish writer, Jöns Budde, lived as a monk. He died in 1491 and his monument is in the graveyard. The church was originally the monastic church, but was drastically altered in 1797 when its orientation was reversed and the cupola, to the design of C. F. Adelcrantz, added to the tower. It has a fine, bold vaulted interior with two aisles, painted white throughout, and a good carved pulpit. No other monastic buildings survive.

4 Later Churches - sixteenth to nineteenth centuries

The late sixteenth-, seventeenth- and early eighteenth-century churches served the Lutheran instead of the Roman Catholic faith, Finland having finally accepted the Reformation in 1527. The sequence of stone-built village churches—Finland's most interesting contribution to medieval architecture—had come to an end and the new churches were of wood; for the Finnish church had become much poorer after Sweden abolished the monastic orders. These churches followed, at first, much the same pattern as the wooden churches of the medieval period, none of which now remain. Architecturally, in fact, Finland emerged from the Middle Ages gradually and late.

In Ostrobothnia especially there was much church-building in the seventeenth century, an activity which spread inland as more of the country acquired a permanent population. But medieval practices in the way of wall and roof construction and of vaulting persisted, as well as the medieval hall-shape and, in some instances, the steep roofs and pinnacled towers. The first signs of a new approach to church design occurred in the second half of the century when centralized or cruciform churches—a Renaissance rather than a medieval conception—began to appear, inspired, it is generally presumed, by St Katherine's Church, Stockholm, designed by Jean de la Valleé in 1656.

From this new approach sprang the numerous cruciform churches —still built of wood—which, by the late eighteenth century, had become the commonest pattern in most parts of Finland, though there were other factors that led towards this plan-shape besides the conscious adoption of the formal geometry of the Renaissance. For example, a cruciform shape was arrived at, as in the case of Keuruu (1756–58), when the sacristy and armoury that projected on either side of the medieval type of church were transformed into a pair of transepts by raising the level of their roofs. There were, at the same time, churches with polygonal eastern ends (a speciality of a leading master-builder, Matti Honka) that also seem to have developed directly from the medieval hall church. Finland being a meeting-ground of the Western and Eastern branches of the Christian Church, it might be supposed that the fashion for centralized church plans was a Byzantine one, due to Russian influence, but there is no evidence that this was so.

Whatever the origin of their new plan-forms, and in spite of variations from region to region, the cruciform churches of the late eighteenth century increasingly conformed to sophisticated fashions in design, the more so as, at the end of the century, professional architects began to take over from the master-builders. One resulting development was the raising of a dome over the crossing, as at Lapua (1827), and another was the introduction of variations on the basic cruciform plan which began with the practice of cutting off the angles, inside and out, and ended in some instances with polygonal plan-forms as at Vimpeli, by Jakob Rijf (1807).

Jakob Rijf was the most creative member of a remarkable family of architect-builders. He was the son of Thomas Rijf, the contractor for Munsala church, designed by C. F. Adelcrantz, a leading Swedish architect, and completed in 1792. Jakob first worked with his father and was then sent by the Swedish king to study architecture at the academy at Stockholm. He was therefore the first native Finn to be trained professionally as an architect. His other works include churches at Larsmo (probably his best) and at Oravainen, an Ostrobothnian village south of Pietarsaari, the latter designed to be built in stone but executed in wood. In 1794–7 he rebuilt, in a quite ambitious Renaissance style, the medieval church at Alatornio.

In eastern Finland there evolved a double-cruciform type of church, the speciality of another family of builders, the Salonens, which may have influenced the ideas of some of the architects who designed neoclassical churches during the Empire period.

The internal arrangement of churches also underwent changes in the course of the seventeenth and eighteenth centuries. The greater emphasis on the pulpit, associated with the Lutheran religion, had its influence, though the medieval choir-screen, an expression of Catholic mystery and ritual, survived in a modified form. Most of the screens were, however, destroyed in the nineteenth century. The practice of painting the walls and ceilings continued, often in the form of simulated architectural embellishments and draperies.

In the later seventeenth century the many-storeyed, free-standing bell-towers that are so characteristic a feature of the Finnish rural landscape first made their appearance. Some of them—those that stand alongside medieval churches—are described and illustrated in the preceding chapter, because church and bell-tower are visually inseparable; the mottled, grey stone walls of the church and the clear smooth colours of the bell-tower's paintwork are essential elements of the village picture. But, chronologically, bell-towers belong to this chapter.

Like the village churches themselves, the bell-towers show variations in design from region to region. In Ostrobothnia, where the first bell-towers were built, the typical pattern has three storeys with an octagonal cupola, and there are similar types in the south west (for example Lohja and Siuntio, already illustrated); in the south the main intermediate floor, which contains the bells, is sometimes octagonal, and in eastern Finland there are late eighteenth-century examples, such as Ruokolahti, in which the whole structure, from top to bottom, is octagonal.

The wooden churches of this period, with their attendant bell-towers, are a remarkable series, unlike anything that other countries can show. Naive and clumsy though some of them are in the handling of the Renaissance idiom by the builders and master-carpenters responsible for them, they yet have the freshness and directness of a true vernacular, a vernacular that was only gradually superseded by the individual architect-designed church, as the so-called Empire style (the style of the period, beginning in 1809, when Finland was a semi-autonomous duchy of the Russian Empire) established itself.

This period, a period also of widespread civic building (see Chapter 6) was dominated by Carl Ludwig Engel, but for some years before he came to Helsinki (that is, while Finland was still under Swedish rule) the leading architects, based on Turku, were already employing a similar late Renaissance or neoclassical idiom. The work of these architects too is dealt with in Chapter 6, but their influence on church design falls within the scope of this chapter. The outstanding example is the church at Hämeenlinna, designed by Louis Jean Desprez in 1798. Though simple, and no doubt intentionally archaic, this cruciform composition with a central rotunda and a tower crowned by a cupola, is, in spite of being an enlargement of an originally circular church, a fully realized architectural invention that owes nothing either to the improvizations of provincial carpenters or to the medieval traditions that had persisted in the Finnish countryside for so long.

The relative independence of Finnish church-building practices from those prevailing in Sweden, in spite of Swedish political and cultural ascendancy, is underlined by the fact that Sweden had no central authority in charge of church-building until 1759, and that even when such an authority had been set up, its influence was limited to fostering a more academic attention to correct architectural style, resulting in little more than the incorporation of classical frontispieces in church elevations and the decorative application inside of classical elements like pilasters and wall-panelling.

A Swedish statute of 1776 forbidding the use of wood for church-building was but little observed, though a few stone churches—the first since the Middle Ages—were built towards the end of the century (Munsala and Kuopio are examples), and the practice of simulating the appearance of masonry in the wall-treatment of wooden churches may have been influenced by this official preference for stone.

Apart from a very few exceptions, like the Desprez church at Hämeenlinna and the churches of Jakob Rijf already referred to, the period of the architect-designed, neoclassical church coincides with the early period of Russian Imperial rule. In 1810, the year after Sweden had yielded up Finland to Russia, a central building organization was set up in Finland. The first head of it—the first

holder of the office of Controller of Public Works—was Carlo Francesco Bassi, an architect of Italian origin who designed a number of churches, a typical example being the Old Church in Tampere (1824). He was succeeded as controller in 1824 by C. L. Engel who had been working on the improvement and rebuilding of Helsinki since 1816.

Under Engel's supervision a great number of neoclassical churches were constructed and bell-towers in the same style were added to existing churches. He was, in the fullest sense, the architect of some of them, including metropolitan examples like the Vanha (Old) Church in Helsinki (1826) and the Lutheran cathedral (1830–40) which dominates the government quarter of the city, and possibly some of the churches in important towns—important, that is, in his day—like Hamina and Lapua. Other churches built under his administration were no doubt the product of ideas and even of drawings issued by his organization; but many of the buildings to which the name of Engel is attached are unlikely to have been designed by him in any more direct sense, judging both by the sheer impossibility of one man producing so many designs in so short a time, and by the inexpert proportions and the unsophisticated, rough-and-ready details of the buildings themselves.

The Finnish churches of this period are nevertheless a remarkable achievement, and the presence, among the low wooden buildings of modest country towns, of ambitious, domed, neoclassical churches and many-storeyed bell-towers is an indication of the energy and administrative skill behind the architectural organization set up by the Imperial regime. This phase, however, lasted but a short time after Engel's death in 1840.

The later nineteenth-century Finnish churches fall into two main categories, the first of which is a direct continuation of what was being done a century before. This consists of wooden churches—they might be termed carpenters' churches whether in fact designed by master-carpenters or by professionally trained architects—resembling the earlier wooden churches but deriving their architectural nature, inside and out, from their vigorous use of carpenter's ornament, often with a Gothic flavour, in the shape of applied pilasters, panelling and mouldings. The result is often somewhat gimcrack and nearly always naive in relation to sophisticated standards of design, but these churches have a positive, idiosyncratic character and were sometimes surprisingly ambitious in scale, as in the case of the vast hill-top edifice at Kerimäki (1848), said to be the largest wooden church in the world.

The other category of later nineteenth-century churches conforms more closely to the eclectic fashions then being followed by architects elsewhere. Their work in Finland was especially influenced from north Germany, for although Finland continued to be a province of the Russian Empire until 1917, little architectural influence came from Russia except into the extreme eastern part of the country. Church architecture, as in other countries, was much influenced by the Gothic Revival, and the neo-Gothic church at Ylistaro, near Vaasa (1847–51) by E. B. Lohrmann, that at Pori (1863) by G. T. Chiewitz (shown on page 56), and that at Vaasa by C. A. Setterberg (1867) may be taken as typical of this period. The Gothic Revival was succeeded, at the end of the century, by the more vigorous and inventive National Romantic style which is separately dealt with in Chapter 9.

Askainen

This is in a village north west of Turku. The simple rectangular church was built in 1653 at the direction of Herman Fleming,

proprietor of the neighbouring country house of Louhisaari (see page 59). The interior still contains his private pew, raised high above the floor of the church, reached by a wooden stair and decorated with his coat-of-arms. The bell-tower in the foreground of the picture—stone-based with a timber superstructure—was added in the eighteenth century. The church is approached through the central arch of the bell-tower.

Tornio

The small town of Tornio, a timber-shipping port, lies right on the Swedish border, at the head of the Gulf of Bothnia, on an island in the river, connected to Sweden by a spit of land and to Finland by a bridge. The church, which has been out of use since 1735, is a remarkable wooden structure with the steep, shingle-covered, pointed roofs typical of Ostrobothnia. Though built by the master-carpenter Matti Härmä (who also worked in Sweden) in 1684–86, it is still in many ways medieval in conception. Inside it has a vaulted wooden ceiling richly painted, with wreaths enclosing circular panels with saints and angels, and a choir-screen and other furnishings carved in 1706 by Nils Fluur, a native of Tornio. The painter was the Danish-born Didrik Möllerum. The bell-tower, the oldest in north Finland, was built in 1687.

Merimasku

Like Askainen, this is one of the ring of old village churches to the west and north of Turku. It is a typical example of the eighteenth-century timber-built church, with classical details but differing very little in its layout from the type that preceded it. Merimasku Church

Tornio church (1684–6) by
Matti Härmä

Tornio church: interior
(furnishings 1706)

Merimasku church (1726)

Pietarsaari church: bell-tower (1761)

is dated 1726. Its boarded walls are stained deep red, with only a few details picked out in white. It has a nice interior with painted marbling on the walls. The timber-built bell-tower can just be seen on the left of the picture.

Pietarsaari (Swedish, Jakobstad)

The church stands near the centre of this substantial town, on the shore of the Gulf of Bothnia, which was founded in the mid-seventeenth century (see also page 98). It was built in 1761. The picture shows the detached bell-tower, with the church itself beyond. Both are wholly of wood and are typical of the church architecture of the region. They are strongly coloured, dark-yellow and white, with shingled roofs.

Keuruu

This is a good example of another common type of eighteenth-century wooden church. It stands in a village 64km (40 miles) to the west of Jyväskylä, and was built, in 1756–8, by Antti Hakola. Simple outside, with somewhat crude attempts at classical embellishments and a two-tiered spired turret surmounting a western tower, it has an unusually charming interior. A west gallery is supported on bulbous columns and a boarded ceiling arches above exposed tie-beams. The ceiling and the gallery-front are decorated with paintings.

Keuruu church (1756-8) by
Antti Hakola

Keuruu church: interior

Petäjävesi church (1763-4)
by Jaakko Leppänen

Petäjävesi

Another simple wooden church with a steep shingled roof, this stands in a village between Keuruu (see page 42) and Jyväskylä. It was built by Jaakko Leppänen in 1763–4, and has a beautifully modelled and furnished interior, lined with boarding.

Nurmo church (1772): bell-tower
in foreground

Munsala church (1777) by
C. F. Adelcrantz

Nurmo

Nurmo is just south of Lapua. The bell-tower here is almost identical with that at Purmo, also in Ostrobothnia, with only minor variations in detail, showing how near-standard designs were evolved, presumably by one master-carpenter. Purmo is known to be by Antti Hakola and to have been completed in 1772, and it is probable that this church is also by him.

The bell-tower stands right on the village street. Note in the photograph, attached to its base, one of the carved, wooden, costumed figures (*vaivaisukko*) holding a collecting-box for the poor, that are found in many of these Ostrobothnian churches. The church itself follows the familiar pattern, with a somewhat more elaborate central cupola over an octagonal structure created by cutting across the internal corners of the basic cruciform plan.

Munsala

This church is of cruciform plan with an attached western tower, in a village on the Gulf of Bothnia, north of Vaasa. The design, made in 1777 by the Swedish architect, C. F. Adelcrantz, marks the first use of stone for the building of churches since the medieval stone churches of the fourteenth and fifteenth centuries. Note also the use of a fairly sophisticated imported Renaissance idiom.

Lappeenranta Orthodox church
(1785)

Lappeenranta Orthodox church:
interior

Hämeenlinna church : south porch

Lappeenranta (Swedish, Villmanstrand)

This is an Orthodox church, one of the few included in this survey since the Greek Orthodox rite was in the main confined to Karelia and other parts of eastern Finland, areas which have been perennially under Russian rule and, because of their nearness to Russia itself, always under Russian influence. Lappeenranta, by the Treaty of Turku signed in 1743 after a Finno-Swedish army had been heavily defeated in a battle nearby, became Russian territory and a fortified frontier town. To the north west of the town are the remains of fortifications built at this time, and the plain, but elegant, classical church, entered through an attached bell-tower, stands among them. The church was built in 1785 and has a simple plan with a barrel-vaulted nave separated from flat-ceilinged aisles by pairs of columns, but the white and gilt interior is given great richness by baroque furnishings and by the gilt-framed paintings displayed all over the walls as well as on the ikonostasis which, as in all Orthodox churches, conceals the sanctuary from the nave.

Hämeenlinna (Swedish, Tavastehus)

Hämeenlinna is a mature, medium-size town 96km (60 miles) north of Helsinki, notable among other things for being the birthplace of Jean Sibelius. The church, the first in Finland in the neoclassical style, was built in 1798 and was designed by Louis Jean Desprez (1737–1804), an architect of French origin who worked in Sweden where he was for a time stage-painter to King Gustav III as well as the king's appointed architect. It is a handsomely modelled stucco-faced building with somewhat archaic detail, precociously Greek in places—for example, the columned porch facing the market square. This was part of the church as first built. It was then circular in plan, with the seating arranged round a central altar, and was so planned at the suggestion of King Gustav III who came back from a visit to Italy with a project to commission churches of the Pantheon type in Sweden and Finland. However, the church at Hämeenlinna was the only one built. The tower and cupola were added in 1837 and the church was enlarged, by Josef Stenbäck, in 1892 to give it its present cruciform shape. It was restored by Aarno Ruusuvuori in 1964.

Hämeenlinna church (1798) by
L. J. Desprez; tower 1837

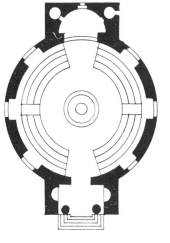

Plan of Hämeenlinna church
before enlargement

47

Lapua church (1827)

Lapua

In the centre of Ostrobothnia, Lapua has been the scene of many important events in Finnish history, political and military. A river, the Lapuanjoki, flows through the town, and beside it stands this large, domed, wooden church by C. L. Engel (or, more likely, by Heikki Kuorikoski, one of the architects in the public works office controlled by him) and its characteristic three-storey bell-tower. The office designed, from 1820 onwards, a number of churches of similar type, but that at Lapua was the first to be completed, in 1827. It has a cruciform plan with a high central octagon and an octagonal dome.

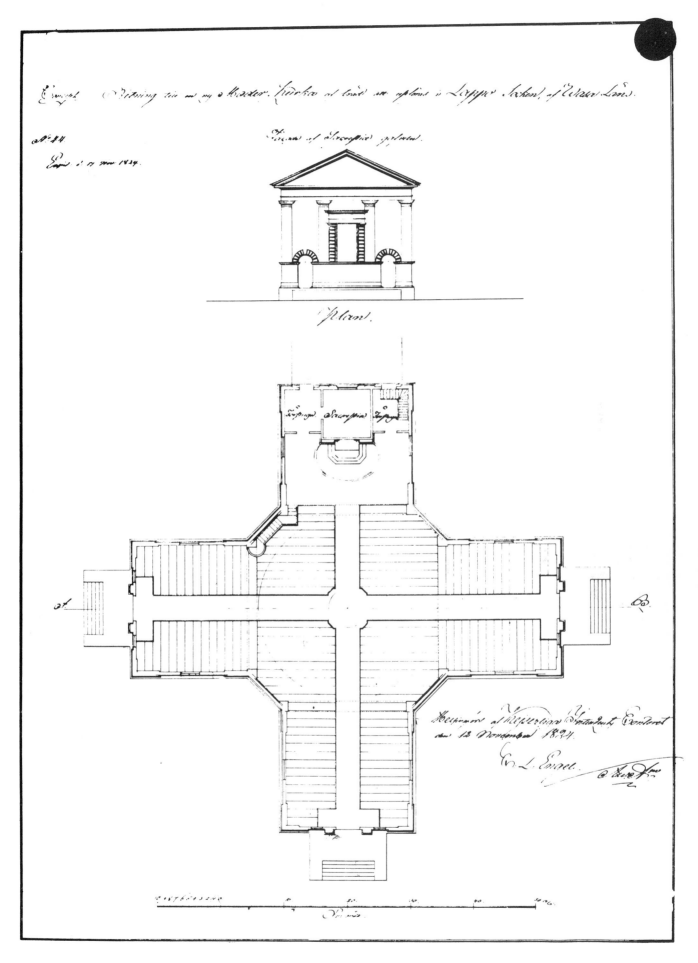

Lapua Church; contemporary
plan signed by Engel

Helsinki. Vanha (old) church
(1826) by C. L. Engel

(right) Plan of Helsinki
cathedral

Tampere old church (1824) by
C. F. Bassi

Tampere (Swedish, Tammerfors)

The Old Church in this, Finland's second city (for the larger and later church—now the cathedral—see Chapter 9, and for the latest see Chapter 11), was designed in 1824 by Carlo Francesco Bassi (1772–1840), the Italian-born architect who came from Stockholm to become Finland's first controller of public works and who gave its neoclassical character to part of Turku (see Chapter 6). The Old Church, which is built of wood, stands at the upper end of the sloping central square. It has the cruciform plan already at that time common in Sweden, and a central dome. Bassi prepared designs for a number of churches of this type, but some were varied in their execution by local builders.

Helsinki (Swedish, Helsingfors)

With the Vanha (Old) Church at Helsinki, we approach the golden age of Finnish civic architecture, when Carl Ludwig Engel adorned Helsinki, after it had become the capital under the new Russian regime, with the formally laid out neoclassical buildings that give so much distinction to the city's government area (see Chapter 6). This church, designed by Engel in 1826 before he began the cathedral, stands somewhat apart from his main group of civic and university buildings of which the cathedral is the centre, since it is on the further side of the central avenue formed by the tree-lined Esplanade and Mannerheimintie, though near their junction. It occupies one corner of a green space between Lönnrotinkatu and Bulevardi and is

Helsinki cathedral (1830-40) by C. L. Engel

a good example of Finnish wooden-church architecture at its most assured and dignified. It is now much used for ceremonial purposes.

The Lutheran cathedral (first called the Nikolai Church) was designed by Engel and built between 1830 and 1840. It dominates Senate Square and the whole government and university area (see Chapter 6) and indeed the city itself when approached from the sea. It stands at the top of a wide flight of steps at the upper end of the sloping square, the steps being terminated at either end by tall pedimented pavilions between which a high platform spans the front of the cathedral's southern portico. This was not, however, as Engel conceived it. He terminated this side of the square with a colonnaded guardhouse (built 1818) above which was the cathedral

platform reached by steps at either end. The guardhouse was replaced by the present wide flight of steps soon after 1840, the year of Engel's death, by E. B. Lohrmann, another German architect who had settled in Finland. He also elaborated the previously very simple structure of the cathedral with four small corner domes, with sculptured figures and with the two side pavilions. Although the building was completed in time to be opened only a few months after Engel's death to celebrate the bicentenary of the founding of the university alongside it, it was not consecrated until 1852. The interior, with its large saucer-dome (restored in 1962) is dull and academic.

Hamina Orthodox church and
bell-tower (1837)

Rautalampi church (1844)

Turku Orthodox church (1846) by C. L. Engel

Hamina (Swedish, Fredrikshamn)

The Orthodox church occupies one of the angles formed by the radiating streets of this remarkably laid out town (see Chapter 6). It is a circular domed building of 1837, in a walled enclosure which is entered through the arched lower storey of a free-standing bell-tower. This has a somewhat fanciful upper storey with steeple and miniature onion dome which give it an appropriately Russian flavour, although it was in fact designed by an Italian architect called Visconti. The combination of its green roofs and pink and white paintwork gives the group of buildings, standing among trees, a toy-like prettiness.

Rautalampi

This is another typical wooden church of the Empire period, attributed to Engel but dated three years after his death and clearly more a product of the office he controlled than of his own pencil because of its strange proportions and inexpert handling of detail. The church is of considerable size for a mere village, and over the west door is a tablet with an inscription recording that it was built in 1844 on the orders of the emperor, Nicholas I. The three-storey bell-tower has a simple rustic charm. Rautalampi is in central Finland between Kuopio and Jyväskylä.

Turku (Swedish, Åbo)

This Orthodox church in Finland's former capital city stands at the highest point of the large central market square. It was designed by C. L. Engel and completed in 1846, after his death: a circular domed building with a Doric portico. It was probably his last personal design.

53

Kerimäki church (1848) by E. B. Lohrmann and A. F. Granstedt

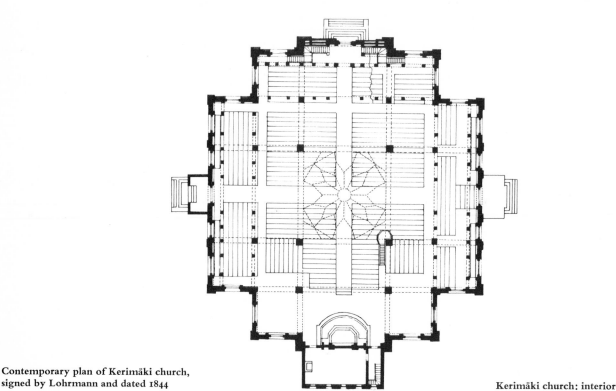

Contemporary plan of Kerimäki church, signed by Lohrmann and dated 1844

Kerimäki church: interior

Kerimäki

This is perhaps the most extraordinary wooden church in Finland. It is of vast size (it claims to be the largest wooden church in the world, and it may well be so; its most likely rivals being the cathedral at Georgetown, Guyana, and the Mormon tabernacle of 1870 at Salt Lake City, with its vast elliptical roof). Kerimäki Church stands on a hilltop in the rolling landscape of eastern Finland, about 24km (15 miles) east of Savonlinna, so that its somewhat ungainly outline can be seen from a great distance. Kerimäki is only a village— though one that serves as the centre of a large rural area—yet the church seats 3,400 people. It was first planned in 1842, by E. B. Lohrmann, to seat 1,500, but the parishioners demanded something larger and A. F. Granstedt (who had been one of Engel's official assistants) was commissioned to provide an enlarged version of the

Lohrmann design. The construction was the work of the parishioners themselves, the only trained craftsman being the builder in charge, and this no doubt explains the odd variations in scale and the naive application of a mixture of classical and Gothic detail. The style as a whole, as well as the cruciform plan, closely resembles that of the mid-century carpenters' churches referred to above.

Kerimäki Church was completed in 1848. The interior is much more successful than the exterior, the sense of space being truly impressive, the lighting well controlled and the ornament more subtly handled. What might appear a somewhat clumsy use of wooden struts and tie-beams in fact adds to the scale and interest of the upper spaces, especially the space, clerestory lit, beneath the central dome. The colour of the interior is also excellent, with light grey paint reinforced by marbling on the columns and pilasters.

Pori (Swedish, Björneborg)

Pori is an ancient town on the Gulf of Bothnia, from which the sea has now receded. It has a geometrical plan, the result of systematic rebuilding after a series of destructive fires, the last in 1852, and a town-hall by Engel, built in 1841. The church, which stands by the bridge across the Kokemäenjoki, exemplifies the historical revivalism that was current all over Europe at the time it was built (1863), but it also retains something in common, notably in its angular Gothic detail, with the carpenters' churches still being built in Finland, in spite of the spire and window-frames being in this case of cast iron—the only example in Finland of the use of this material for such purposes.

The architects were G. T. Chiewitz and C. T. von Heideken. Chiewitz (1815–62) was a leading architect around the middle of the nineteenth century. He first practised in Sweden and came to Finland in 1851, where his most important building was the House of the Nobility in Helsinki (pages 88-9). In 1860 he became town architect

of Turku, but he died two years later. Von Heideken, who completed the church after Chiewitz's death, was also the architect of the country house at Tjusterby shown on page 66.

Kajaani

This is a typical instance of the tradition of carpenters' churches being carried on by the professional architects. Built as late as 1896 by J. Ahrenberg, it has a wholly consistent interior, all in wood, with columns, boarded ceilings and a hammer-beam roof as well as a full complement of furniture: pews, north gallery and pulpit are shown in the photograph. The style, as one would expect so late in the century, is more Gothic than in the earlier carpenters' churches, with evidence of German influence. Kajaani is an industrial town on Lake Oulujärvi in north-central Finland, on the main road leading up to Lapland. The town was founded by Per Brahe in 1651. It has a town-hall (1831) attributed to Engel; also the ruins of a castle (see Chapter 2).

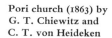

**Pori church (1863) by
G. T. Chiewitz and
C. T. von Heideken**

(right)
**Kajaani church (1898) by
J. Ahrenberg: interior**

5 Country Houses

Finland, as the opening chapter of this book explains, has never been a country of feudal castles and aristocratic mansions, and country houses of a more modest kind were relatively few. The earlier examples, built of logs, were little different from farmhouses, and while the rest of northern Europe was cultivating, from the seventeenth century onwards, a form of civilization based largely on country-house life and the power that resided there, Finland built few such houses of any architectural pretension. Louhisaari (1655), near Turku, is one example that survives of the square symmetrical Renaissance-style mansion; others are Sjundby, also illustrated here, and Degerby at Loviisa. These, it may be noted, are in regions primarily Swedish in language and allegiance.

Even such aristocratic or manorial life as there was vanished in the eighteenth century when Finland was torn by wars and occupied by Russian troops, and the Swedish nobility who owned estates there were recalled to Sweden by royal command. Not till the end of the century, when conditions became more settled, were country houses built again, this time chiefly for the merchant class; the Swedish aristocracy did not, except in a few areas, re-establish itself on the land. The leading architect who specialized at this time in country houses was the German-born C. F. Schröder who worked in Turku. Among the mansions he designed was Fagervik, in the southern province of Uusimaa. This was the centre of a complex of buildings serving the iron industry (see page 60).

There was a second period of country-house building at the beginning of the nineteenth century. Carlo Francesco Bassi, the Italian-born architect who was Finland's first Controller of Public Works, designed a number, and his successor, Carl Ludwig Engel—the dominating architectural figure of the Russian regime that began in 1809—was nearly as prolific in his output of country houses as he was of town-halls and churches. These were seldom, however, on the palatial scale of the great country houses built elsewhere in Europe, the only Finnish mansion that compared with even the lesser of these being Mon Repos, a wooden neoclassical mansion, designed by Engel, in a landscaped park outside Viipuri—and thus no longer in Finland. Otherwise the Finnish country houses, which are most often of wood and are chiefly to be found in southern and western Finland, especially in the traditionally Swedish-speaking areas are best compared with the Queen Anne or Georgian mansions of country squires in England, being modest in scale and serving also as the administrative centre for large agricultural estates.

Louhisaari (Swedish, Villnäs)

The best surviving example of the seventeenth-century Finnish country house. It is situated north west of Turku and was built for his own occupation in 1655 by Herman Fleming who also built the Askainen village church at the park gates (see page 40). The house is planned—as was common at the time—with low out-buildings enclosing an entrance forecourt (the photograph is taken from the opposite side). The ground floor of the main block contains the domestic offices, the family living rooms are on the first floor and the main reception rooms on the top floor. Louhisaari is notable for having been the birthplace (in 1867) of Marshal Mannerheim whose family had acquired it at the end of the eighteenth century. It is now a museum devoted to his memory.

Sarvlax

This was originally a similar house to Louhisaari, having been built in 1683; but it was largely redesigned in the 1880s by F. A. Sjöström and its façades, with pilasters rising through its three storeys and a heavy cornice, belong to this time. The loggia on the garden side, seen in the photograph, is later still. Only the small pediment survives from the seventeenth-century exterior.

Sarvlax is near the village of Pernaja, just east of Porvoo, and in the graveyard of the small, medieval Pernaja Church is a sepulchral chapel belonging to the Creutz, von Morian and von Born families, successive owners of the Sarvlax estate. This chapel is a handsome Greek Revival structure of 1834, designed by Pehr Granstedt.

Sjundby

This is a simpler, less sophisticated, stone-built country mansion west of Helsinki, also of the seventeenth century. It has walls of uncoursed boulders, partly plastered, similar to those of many medieval churches, and a cut-stone doorway. The main reception rooms are on the first floor.

Louhisaari (1655) from the park

Sarvlax (1683; remodelled c 1880): garden side

Sjundby (seventeenth century)

Fagervik (1773) by C. F. Schröder

Fagervik

A well preserved example of the eighteenth-century country house, this formed the centre of a self-contained iron-working estate, employing waterpower from the lake beside which the proprietor's mansion stands. It is near the village of Inkoo, west of Helsinki. The estate is approached up a narrow lane lined on either side with the small, red-painted wooden houses of the iron-workers (one of which can be seen in the bottom righthand corner of the picture) together with a village shop and school. At the top of the lane is the church with its detached bell-tower, also of wood, painted red, and beyond them is the house itself, laid out in traditional form with low outbuildings enclosing a gravelled forecourt. The church was built by J. F. Schultz in 1737 and the bell-tower added in 1766.

The house is by C. F. Schröder, and is dated 1773. It has three storeys, the upper of which is partly in a central pedimented pavilion and partly in a mansard roof. The ironworks themselves are in a valley south of the village.

Fagervik estate, with church (1730), bell-tower (1766) and house in background

Mustio (Swedish, Svartå)

Here is another example of a mansion planned as the centre of an iron-working estate, in this case at Karjaa, near the south coast and west of Helsinki. The air-view shows the layout of the whole complex, with the pedimented mansion in the centre, the church in the foreground and the lake, with its sluices providing water-power, on the right. The mansion was first designed in 1783 by the same architect, C. F. Schröder, who designed Fagervik, and then somewhat altered in 1791 by the Stockholm architect, Erik Palmstedt.

Mustio estate, with house (1783)
by C. F. Schröder in centre

Orisberg (1804) from the lake

Orisberg

Built in 1804, this Ostrobothnian country house, a few kilometres east of Vaasa, stands in a wooded park with its garden side facing a lake, from the edge of which the photograph is taken. The shores of the lake are furnished with a classical pavilion and a water-mill.

Viurila

This is near the village of Halikko, 169km (105 miles) west of Helsinki: the centre of one of several large agricultural estates in this region. The simple pedimented house, of two storeys plus an attic, was designed by C. F. Bassi in 1804–11. Its highly monumental stables, using a Greek Doric order resembling that at Paestum, were added by C. L. Engel in the 1840s.

Viurila (1804-11) by C. F. Bassi

Viurila: the stables (*c* 1840) by
C. L. Engel

Vuojoki (1836) by C. L. Engel

Tjusterby (1867) by
C. T. von Heideken

66

Noormarkku. Ahlström house (1877)

Vuojoki

One of the largest country houses of the Empire period, this was designed by C. L. Engel and completed in 1836. It is in southern Ostrobothnia, just north of Rauma, and consists of a main three-storey block flanked by single-storey pilastered pavilions which are placed in line with it instead of being brought forward, as in the earlier houses, to enclose a forecourt.

Tjusterby

This house is unusual in several ways: for its late date (1867) and for being built of red brick, in a romantic style with a Gothic flavour. It was designed by C. T. von Heideken—a pupil of Chiewitz for whom he completed the church at Pori (see page 56). It is not far from the village of Pernaja, and, therefore, from Sarvlax (see page 58), and stands in a beautifully wooded estate of some

antiquity, containing farm buildings dating back to the early eighteenth century.

Noormarkku

This is an all-timber mansion, near Pori, with the elaborate carpenter's ornament and romantic outline of its period. It was built in 1877 for Antti Ahlström, a leading industrialist, and is still used by his descendants. The interior and its furnishings have been preserved almost unchanged. The house stands in a large wooded park which also contains an ironworks and several other and later houses, each built for a different member of the Ahlström family. The latest of these is the Villa Mairea (see page 150), designed in 1937 by Alvar Aalto for Antti Ahlström's grand-daughter, Maire Gullichsen.

6 Civic Buildings - eighteenth and nineteenth centuries

In the past Finland was never a nation of town dwellers. Even as recently as the beginning of the sixteenth century there were only two towns in the whole country that deserved the name—Turku and Viipuri—and Viipuri (which is in the territory ceded to Russia in 1940 and is therefore outside the scope of this book) was the only town protected by walls. In the succeeding centuries town life developed but slowly, and civic buildings of any pretension (as well as large commercial buildings, which are also included in the present chapter) were thus, in Finland, a relatively late development.

A few old towns, like Porvoo and Rauma, retain modest eighteenth-century civic buildings in their centres, and there are some isolated public buildings of this period elsewhere; but the first group of civic buildings on an urban scale is at Turku, built soon after 1800. These were followed twenty years later by the splendid array of government and university buildings, designed by C. L. Engel, which give the area of Helsinki that rises behind the waterfront of the South Harbour so distinguished an air, and by a number of isolated buildings, mostly the work of Engel or his official associates, in provincial towns. Finally, from the early period there is the exceptional military town of Hamina, with its formal layout radiating from a neoclassical town-hall. Public buildings in most other Finnish towns belong to periods after the neoclassical style of the early nineteenth century had decayed, but continue for the most part to employ some form of Renaissance idiom.

In spite of the short time during which the purer neoclassical style (also called the Empire style because of its association with the Imperial Russian regime) was current, it constitutes one of the outstanding episodes in the history of Finnish architecture, largely because of the quality of Engel's Helsinki buildings which arose as part of the total reconstruction of Helsinki under the new Russian regime. But, before this was undertaken, Turku had built the first of a number of handsome buildings in similar style, though with a somewhat different flavour, the earliest dating from the time, just before the Napoleonic wars, when Finland was still under the rule of Sweden.

The neoclassical buildings in Turku, although they provide the red-brick, medieval cathedral with its agreeable setting of cream and white stucco, half concealed by greenery, are fragmentary compared with those in Helsinki because of the sequence of catastrophes that Turku suffered during the time when they were being built. The first of these was the removal of the seat of government from Turku to Helsinki in 1812, three years after Finland had become a grand duchy of the Russian Empire. The decision was made by the Emperor Alexander I with the object of bringing the capital further away from Sweden and its influence. The second catastrophe, in 1827, was a disastrous fire—the worst that has ever been experienced by a north-European city—and the third, a direct consequence of the fire, was the removal of the university to Helsinki in 1828. Losing its medieval street pattern and its status as a government and academic centre, as well as its population of officials, professors and students, Turku had to change its nature within a generation into that of an almost wholly mercantile centre, which it remains to this day in spite of now possessing its own university once more—in fact two universities: a Swedish-speaking and a Finnish.

The town was rebuilt to a more spacious and regular pattern devised by Engel, and the park-like setting of the buildings round the cathedral, which replaced densely-packed medieval houses, dates from this time. In the same area also stands the most important neoclassical building from before the fire: the Old University building. Its architect was Carl Christoffer Gjörwell (1766-1837); but he was at the same time city architect of Stockholm and could not come to Finland to supervise the work. So he sent his assistant, Carlo Francesco Bassi (1772-1840), who stayed to become Turku's leading architect.

Bassi was born in Turin, came to Sweden at the age of eleven, studied architecture at the academy and, after a brief return to Italy, joined Gjörwell's office. The teacher of both of them was Desprez (see page 47), King Gustav III's favourite architect. The Old University building was not completed until 1815, after Finland had been ceded to Russia and was cut off from Sweden; so it can be regarded as more Bassi's work than Gjörwell's. At the same time he designed the country house at Viurila shown on page 65. In 1810 he had been appointed by the Russian administration to the new office of Controller of Public Works for Finland, but by the time building started again after the war he was already becoming overshadowed by Engel.

The other leading architect of Turku was Pehr Johan Gylich, also Swedish-trained, who served as city architect from 1829–59. He and Bassi evolved the characteristic Turku version of the neoclassical style with its pilastered or porticoed façades, sometimes richly modelled as in the case of the residence of the Hjelt family designed by Gylich in 1831, and these, along with Engel's layout and a few isolated buildings like the grammar school (formerly the Court of Appeal) and the Swedish Theatre, furnish Turku with what civic distinction it has retained.

The civic history of Helsinki begins as that of Turku declines. When it became the capital in 1812 Helsinki was an unimportant town with a population of only 4,000. The Russians occupied it early in the war of 1808–9 and in the former year it was severely damaged by a fire nearly as disastrous as that at Turku. Rebuilding plans were drawn up by a Lieutenant Kocke, but before these could be carried out the decision was taken to make Helsinki the capital and new plans were made, of a more revolutionary and far-sighted kind, on the orders of Alexander I, said to be with the object of exhibiting the magnanimity and the civilizing intentions of the new regime.

The author of the new town plan, which was finalized in 1817, was Johan Albert Ehrenström, a politician and amateur of the arts, who presided over the reconstruction committee for fourteen years. His plan was grand in scale and classical in conception, and central Helsinki as it appears at present, with the wide Esplanade running westwards from the South Harbour and the spaciously laid out squares and terraces of monumental buildings climbing the slope to the north and dominated by the cathedral, derives from it. The predominantly three-storey buildings in the centre gave way to lower wooden buildings in the surrounding residential quarters, all likewise neoclassical in their proportions and details, set among gardens as they became more widely spaced at the outer edge of the city.

Helsinki has been continuously extended, modernized and rebuilt, but the central area of 1817–40 remains virtually intact and furnishes some indication of the marvellous sight it must have afforded a century and a half ago: a model city, all of a piece in its layout and its architecture, light in tone since it was wholly of painted wood and stucco, expertly set into its rocky landscape penetrated by arms of the sea, ice-bound or in sparkling movement according to the season. Its creation was a remarkable achievement in that time and place, and in the space of a single generation.

The achievement as we now see it lies, however, not so much in Ehrenström's plan which, though far-sighted and ambitious, was a conventional product of its time, showing the French influence then predominant in Sweden; it lies rather in the architecture by Engel that gave the plan three-dimensional form. Ehrenström's greatest service to Finland was the invitation, issued to Engel by him and his reconstruction committee in 1815, to come to Helsinki from St Petersburg and take architectural charge of the new capital.

Carl Ludwig Engel (1778–1840) had, in fact, then been in St Petersburg for only a year, although that city's neoclassical architecture had a profound and lasting influence on him. He was of German origin, having been born in Berlin where he studied architecture at the *Bauakademie* under Friedrich Gilly and was a contemporary of Schinkel. In 1806 he became town architect of Tallinn, capital of Esthonia, and it was from there that he moved to St Petersburg. He never afterwards travelled in Europe, or indeed left Finland after he had settled in Helsinki where he worked for the remainder of his life—another twenty-five years.

The influence of St Petersburg is especially evident in Engel's earlier buildings in Helsinki, like the guards' barracks in Kasarmitori with their crisply modelled surface decoration; it is seen as well in his skilful subordination of the architectural features to the unity of the whole. His first building after his appointment in 1816 as architect to Helsinki's reconstruction committee—in the activities of which two successive Russian emperors, Alexander I and Nicholas I, took a personal interest—was the naval barracks on Katajanokka peninsula east of the South Harbour. These are plain buildings but finely scaled. They are now disused, but there are plans, drawn up by the architect Erik Kråkström, to convert them into a new foreign ministry, a project on which the Finnish Government hopes to start work in 1980.

Also in 1816 Engel rebuilt the Bock House, the largest private mansion in Helsinki, as a temporary residence for the governor-general, adding its Ionic frontispiece. It stands next to the Sederholm House (page 77) on the south side of Senate Square and the Emperor Alexander I stayed there when he paid his State visit to inspect the progress of the new capital in 1819. It was afterwards for a time the town-hall and now houses magistrates' courts. Engel next embarked on his great complex of buildings surrounding the rest of Senate Square, beginning with the Senate House (1818) on the eastern side. On the removal of the university from Turku to Helsinki in 1827, it was given a site in the square, on the side opposite the Senate House, which had been allocated in Ehrenström's plan to the governor-general's residence. Here Engel built the main university building and, subsequently, adjoining it on the north, the university library and hospital. Finally, as the climax to the whole composition, he built the cathedral—already described on page 51.

The reconstruction committee had been dissolved in 1823, and Engel had then considered leaving Finland and returning to Germany. But he was given an indication that Bassi might soon retire from the office of Controller of Public Works, which office had already, in 1821, been moved from Turku to Helsinki. Bassi did in fact retire in 1824 and moved back to Turku where he designed a number of important buildings following the fire that destroyed much of the city in 1827, and Engel succeeded him as Controller, a post he retained until his death in 1840.

Engel designed many other public buildings in Helsinki, including the Old Church (page 50), the Holy Trinity (Russian Orthodox) church, just north of the cathedral (1826), the city hall (1833), facing the South Harbour (first built as a hotel, see page 82); the guards' barracks already mentioned (1825), of which only one block survives (the remainder having been destroyed by bombing in the last war), the permanent residence of the governor-general (1824) in the Esplanade (now a State banqueting house) and the observatory. The last stands on a hill at the southern end of Unioninkatu which runs at right angles to the Esplanade (the tree-lined avenue leading down to the South Harbour) and thus gives its second formal axis to Ehrenström's plan.

Outside Helsinki Engel, or the office he controlled, produced formal plans for a number of Finnish towns which they also embellished with town-halls and other civic buildings. Pori, Lappeenranta, Kajaani and Kokkola have town-halls to which Engel's name is attached, and he was also responsible for the observatory at Turku (1818), the central part of the old grammar school at Kuopio (1825) and the museum at Tampere, originally a government granary (page 84). Some of the numerous churches designed by him and his office, and the part they played in the evolution of Finnish church architecture, were described in Chapter 4.

Except for a hard, unworkable granite, Finland lacks building stone and all Engel's buildings are of brick or timber covered with plaster, a form of construction of which he had had experience both at Tallinn and at St Petersburg. From these cities, no doubt, he also derived the practice of painting his façades in strong colours with the details picked out in white. The yellow and white of the Senate Building at Helsinki is a vivid and successful example.

One other Helsinki architect of this time should be mentioned: Pehr Granstedt (1764–1828) who designed the large private Heidenstrauch House (now the President's palace) facing the South Harbour in 1818. It was acquired by the State in 1837 and remodelled by Engel as a palace for the Russian Emperor. It is a plain but suitably monumental neoclassical building with a central pediment supported on columns, and forms, with Engel's city-hall and several later buildings, a continuous architectural wall that furnishes both a dignified background to the bustle of the market square and, in the more distant view, a base to the sequence of monumental buildings, crowned by the cathedral, climbing the slope behind.

From the decline of the ubiquitous neoclassical idiom around the middle of the nineteenth century, until National Romanticism gave its new twist to architectural aspirations at the beginning of the twentieth, Finnish architects and their patrons exhibited their skill at historical reminiscence much as they did elsewhere in Europe. Yet the feeling for classical form survived, as did a degree of skill and confidence in handling the Renaissance idiom. The influence of the Gothic Revival was less strongly felt, except in church architecture.

The mid-nineteenth century was not a period of great building activity; it was the time of the Crimean War, of political repression, of famines and social stagnation. But after 1862, when a more liberal political regime coincided with the building of railways and a consequent expansion of commercial activity, towns began to play a more dominant part in Finnish life and large urban buildings of many kinds—offices, stores, theatres, warehouses—were newly in demand. They began the process, which is still continuing today, of replacing with substantial multi-storey structures the low wooden buildings that had hitherto occupied the centres of all the towns.

These new civic and commercial buildings, mostly of brick and plaster but sometimes still of wood, usually employed a Renaissance idiom of a kind. It was sometimes fairly ornate, but even so the

flatness of surface and the overall simplicity of geometrical form which are common to all the preceding eras of Finnish architecture were generally maintained. At this time, also, Finland embarked on the gradual process of industrialization, its start being marked by an ambitious industrial exhibition—similar to those held in London, Paris and elsewhere—at Helsinki in 1876. Significantly, though, the specially constructed exhibition hall was wholly of wood.

Up until Engel's death, the office of the Controller of Public Works, of which he was in charge for sixteen years, served as the principal nursery of young architects. Afterwards the leading architects were mostly Stockholm-trained: for example Chiewitz whose work has already been referred to (page 56), and Carl Theodor Höijer (1843–1910), the outstanding architect of large commercial buildings in the 1880s and the architect also of the National Gallery of Art (Ateneum) in 1887. Finland acquired its own architectural school when the Polytechnic Institute was set up in Helsinki in 1872.

After the end of the century, Finnish architecture was dominated by the, in many ways unique, National Romantic Movement which is the subject of Chapter 9. This, and the Arts and Crafts and Art Nouveau influences associated with it, opened the door to modern architecture, which is dealt with in its experimental phases in Chapter 10 and in its post-war maturity in the last chapter of all. But the eclectic styles continued to have a place in Finnish architecture until at least the 1930s, as they did in that of other countries during the years when modern architectural principles were gradually asserting themselves. In Finland they were thrown even further into the background by the completeness with which National Romanticism dominated the scene in the early years of the century. The continued employment of reminiscent or historical styles during the twentieth century can appropriately be recorded in this chapter because it perpetuated a mode of architectural thinking characteristic of the nineteenth century, and it can be adequately represented by a couple of instances: the theatre at Tampere and the Parliament building at Helsinki (1927–31), the most prominent, and indeed a formidable, example of that tasteful but often somewhat emasculated classicism with which Sweden endowed the world of architectural fashion for a whole generation between the wars.

Porvoo. Old town hall (1764)

70

Rauma. Old town hall (1776)

Porvoo (Swedish, Borgå)

The old town-hall, built in 1764, occupies one side of a cobbled square in the old part of the town not far from the medieval church (see pages 28-9). The main façade is colour-washed terra-cotta, with details picked out in white. In this building the first Finnish diet met in 1809 to proclaim the union between Russian and Finland—never, however, to be summoned again until 1863 (see page 91). The building is now a museum with—as in the case of Rauma—admirably arranged rooms illustrating local life and history.

Rauma

The eighteenth-century town-hall of Rauma, an ancient seaport on the Gulf of Bothnia (see also page 99), was built in 1776 and faces the market square. It is now the town museum.

Hamina. Centre of town from the air

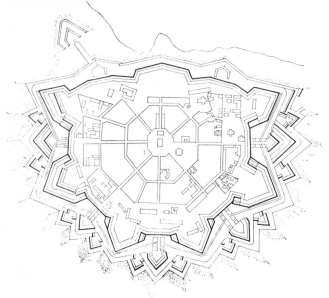

Hamina: town plan showing original fortifications

Hamina (Swedish, Fredrikshamn)

This is the last coastal town on the Gulf of Finland before the Russian frontier, which lies 45km (28 miles) to the east. The earlier town on the site was destroyed during the Russian occupation of 1713–21, but was rebuilt after the Treaty of Uusikaupunki, signed in 1721, which ceded parts of eastern Finland to Russia, making Hamina a frontier town. It was then fortified. After the 1741–3 war, it became Russian territory again and remained so until the whole of Finland became a Russian grand duchy in 1809—in fact for three years longer, since the ceded territories were not reincorporated in the duchy until 1812.

It was during the period of fortification by the Swedes, after 1721, that Hamina was given its geometrical street layout, consisting of a series of concentric octagons linking the streets that radiate from an octagonal central place—a layout that still exists, though it is not so evident on the ground as it is in the aerial view because the varying heights of buildings, and certain cleared spaces, make its symmetry incomplete. The plan is variously attributed to Carl A. Blaesingh and to Axel Löwen. In the middle of the central octagon stands the town-hall, a rectangular pedimented building of 1798 by Brockman, with an octagonal tower and a two-stage turret added by C. L. Engel when he restored the building in 1840 after one of those destructive fires of which Finnish towns were so often the victims. On the north-west side of the square is the Lutheran church (also by Engel), a plain rectangular building without a tower, completed in 1843. On the opposite side is the Orthodox church in its tree-planted compound (pages 52–3)—also seen in the photograph of the town-hall—and further to the east is the Reserve Officers' Training School, whose main building is shown on page 92. Near the market square, which lies to the west of the town centre, is a little octagonal, two-storey building, the so-called Flag Tower, with a curvilinear roof. It was constructed in 1790 on one of the bastions of the fortifications.

Old Vaasa

This court-house (now a church) is all that remains—except for one stone house beside the road about half a kilometre away—of the original town of Vaasa, which was founded by King Charles IX in 1606, near the castle of Korsholm. It was a prosperous trading town, but in 1852 it was completely destroyed by fire except for these two buildings. The ruins of the parish church can also be seen and a few stones marking the site of the castle. The town was rebuilt 7km (4.5 miles) nearer the sea, with a spacious layout by the architect

Carl Axel Setterberg (1812–71) (see page 87) and its Finnish name was changed officially to Nikolainkaupunki, although in practice the old name of Vaasa continued to be used and was officially re-adopted after the Russian Revolution of 1917.

The Old Vaasa Appeal Court had been founded in 1776 by King Gustav III. The court house was designed in 1786 by the Swedish architect, C. F. Adelcrantz (1716–93). After the fire it was converted into a church to serve the neighbouring village of Mustasaari (the name borne by Vaasa in the Middle Ages). The architect for the conversion (1862) was Erkki Kuorikoski who added a bell-tower, just visible in the picture behind the building.

(*above*)
**Old Vaasa. Court house (1786)
by C. F. Adelcrantz;
remodelled as a church (1862)**

(*right*)
**Hamina town hall (1798) by
Brockman; tower (1840) by
C. L. Engel**

Turku. Old University building (1802-15) by C. F. Bassi

Turku (Swedish, Åbo)

The Old University building (1802–15) was designed by Christoffer Gjörwell, the Stockholm city architect, and C. F. Bassi. It was the first of the group of neoclassical civic buildings surrounding Turku Cathedral and, with its plain wall surfaces unbroken by columns or pilasters, and its general severity of style, it presents something of a contrast to the style evolved, in the decades that followed, by Bassi and P. J. Gylich in Turku and by Engel in Helsinki. It has a central assembly hall with columns of polished red granite and an elaborately ornamented, vaulted, plaster ceiling. The hall is now used for concerts; the remainder of the building serves as the Appeal Court. The low building on the left of the picture, known as the Provincial

Governor's Storehouse, is also by Bassi and was built in 1828. Until the beginning of 1977 it was a post office.

The main building of the present *Åbo Akademi* (the Swedish-language university) stands to the west of the Old University building and was formerly the residence of the Trapp family. It was designed by Bassi in 1832-3. Further to the left in the same photograph is another house of about the same date, by P. J. Gylich. The next photograph shows another of the buildings (probably also by Gylich) around the cathedral. It was built in 1829-31 and houses one of the faculties of the *Åbo Akademi*.

Turku. *Åbo Akademi* main
building (1832–3) by C. F. Bassi

Turku. Faculty building,
Åbo Akademi (1829–31)

Raahe. Old customs house (1810)

Raahe (Swedish, Brahestad)

The old customs house at Raahe, a town on the Gulf of Bothnia, founded in 1649 by Per Brahe. The town was of great importance as a centre of shipping during the nineteenth century (see also page 96). The customs house, which now houses an excellent local museum, was built in 1810, immediately after a fire which destroyed much of the town. It is a square, symmetrical, weather-boarded building, standing by the edge of the water which, however, is no longer deep enough for shipping, the sea having retreated all along this coast.

Helsinki (Swedish, Helsingfors)

Sederholm House at the south-east corner of Senate Square was built as a private residence in 1757. It is the oldest surviving building in Helsinki which was but a small country town until it was made the capital after Finland had been ceded by Sweden to Russia.

The neoclassical building at the corner of the Esplanade and Unioninkatu (known as the Uschakoff building, being so named after the Russian-born merchant Jegor Uschakoff who commissioned the first part) was, belying its unified exterior, built in several stages. The nearest part, with central pediment, is by Pehr Gransdtedt (1816), the middle part by C. L. Engel (before 1822) and the far part, repeating the design of the near part, by A. F. Grandstedt (1837). Inside the earliest part is a banking hall installed in 1906, which is one of the most successful of Lars Sonck's National Romantic interiors (see page 122).

Helsinki. Sederholm House,
Senate Square (1757)

Helsinki. Uschakoff Building,
Esplanade (1816-37)

Helsinki. Senate Square (1816-40)
by C. L. Engel

Senate Square, shown here in an air photograph, is the centre of the government area planned by Ehrenström when Helsinki was made the capital of Finland in 1812 and was built by C. L. Engel. It measures about 170m (560ft) by 100m (330ft) and slopes from north to south. At the top of the slope stands the Lutheran cathedral (see page 51), on a platform reached by a flight of steps. These, together with the pavilions at either end, were added in the 1840s (a few years after Engel's death), replacing a colonnaded guardhouse. In the centre of the square is a bronze monument (1894) to the Emperor Alexander II, the most liberal of the Russian emperors and the most sympathetic towards Finnish aspirations.

The Senate House (now the Council of State building), occupying the whole of the east side of the square, was Engel's first large civic building in Helsinki. It was built in 1818-22. The four-storey frontage to the square, which has a central Corinthian portico embracing the two upper storeys (next photograph), is returned round the corner of Aleksanterinkatu on the south to form the end pavilion of the south façade. The same form of pavilion is repeated at the other end, and between them is a two-storey wing with Ionic pilasters and, in the centre, Ionic columns and a pediment marking the entrance. The eastern wing of this large range of buildings—a

Helsinki. Senate House (1818-22)
by C. L. Engel

hollow square in plan—was not completed until 1826 and a northern wing was added after Engel's death. The Senate House has a vaulted staircase with Doric columns.

Opposite the Senate House, on the west side of the square, is the main university building (C. L. Engel, 1828–32). It originally consisted of a square central block with staircase hall in front, semicircular auditorium behind and four-storey wings on either side, but additions were later made at the rear and the auditorium was destroyed by bombing in 1944. It was rebuilt and at the same time enlarged. The original three-storey staircase hall, with galleries supported on Doric columns, survives.

The University Library (1836–45), facing the western side of the cathedral, contains three reading-rooms, the main central one having a shallow domed roof with clerestory lighting and a gallery resting on Corinthian columns. The richly modelled ceilings and vaults had further decoration added to them by F. A. Sjöström in 1879, and an extension was built at the back (G. Nyström) in 1906. Externally the building has a giant order of Corinthian pilasters with semicircular openings in the attic storey above the cornice at either end, providing clerestory lighting to the two small reading-rooms.

Senate Square slopes down towards the Market Square beside

Helsinki's South Harbour, separated from it first by the various
buildings that form the south side of the square (which are smaller
in scale than the others, since they are a survival of the pre-Engel
town, and include the eighteenth-century Sederholm House shown
on page 77 and secondly by the even-fronted line of buildings facing
the harbour. These are—from left to right in the photograph on
page 82—the recently reconverted city hall by Engel (1833); a smaller
neoclassical building, originally a hotel, by Pehr Granstedt (1815);
the Swedish Embassy by Torben Grut (1922); the Supreme Court,
by F. A. Sjöström (1883). Hidden by the last is the President's
Palace referred to on page 70. The low projecting wings that enclose
its forecourt can just be seen. Further to the right, standing high
above the neck of land that joins the Katajanokka peninsula to the
mainland (and therefore separates the South from the North
Harbour) is the tall brick mass, surmounted by gilded domes, of the
Uspenski Orthodox Cathedral, by A. N. Gornostajeff (1868).

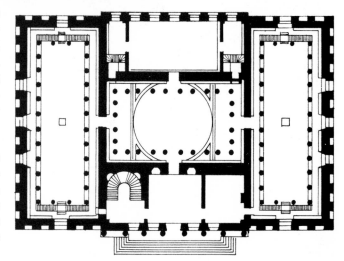

The guards' barracks, built in Kasarmitori by Engel in 1822, of which a large part was destroyed in the last war, is one of the few Engel buildings to be enriched externally by sculptured ornament—in this case military insignia and trophies set into panels or projecting from the wall surface.

Lappeenranta (Swedish, Villmanstrand)

This flourishing town in eastern Finland, on rising ground above Lake Saimaa, became a Russian frontier town after 1743. In Kauppakatu, the street that connects the lake shore with the green space on which stands the town church (one of the wooden churches of Salonen, a master-builder active in east Finland, built in 1795 and with a tower added in 1856) is a modest but neatly designed town-hall—a single-storey weather-boarded building with a clock-turret as high as itself. It was built in 1829, when the town began to move from the garrison area to its present position. Until 1890 the town market occupied the space, now a garden, between the building and the street. The town-hall was the work of a surveyor, J. W. Palmroth, who is known to have based his design on drawings from a volume of type designs issued from the public works office of which Engel had charge—an indication of the way Engel spread his architectural style and standards to the remotest corners of Finland; also of the way buildings attributed to him were often, in fact, only his designs at, as it were, several removes.

Pori (Swedish, Björneborg)

This ancient seaport town in Satakunta, on the Gulf of Bothnia, established on its present site in 1558, possesses a number of distinguished public buildings, placed among wide tree-lined avenues. The town-hall with its handsome pedimented frontispiece is by

Helsinki: South Harbour

Helsinki. Guards' Barracks,
Kasarmitori Square (1822) by
C. L. Engel

Lappeenranta. Town hall (1829)
by J. W. Palmroth

83

Pori. Town Hall (1841) by C. L. Engel

C. L. Engel and was built in 1841. Its roof-turret, surrounded by an iron-railed observation gallery, was added later.

Close to the town-hall stands a large mansion, unusual both for its style and its pretensions, which is now used as municipal offices. It was built in 1895 by a wealthy industrialist called Junnelius who had sought permission to marry the daughter of another wealthy family and had been challenged by her parents to show his ability to provide for her properly. The architect he chose was A. Krook whom he sent on a visit to Venice as preparation for the task—a visit whose results are very evident in the elaborate brick and stone exterior.

Tampere (Swedish, Tammerfors)

This government granary in the city of Tampere is an example of Engel's work at its most severe and functional. Nevertheless the Soane-like modelling of each elevation and the low-pitched roof with lantern give dignity to a very plain brick structure. It was built in 1838 and now houses the Art Museum. Alongside it is a hollow

square of wooden dwellings which are to be preserved as a sample of the town housing of the early nineteenth century.

Loviisa

The town-hall, occupying the centre of one side of the long, tree-planted market square, is a transitional building, preserving the simple geometrical form of the neoclassical period but incorporating eclectically chosen details, some with a Gothic flavour, and surmounted by a picturesque Italianate tower. It was designed in 1856 by G. T. Chiewitz.

Loviisa is an agreeable town and summer resort at the head of a gulf, the entrance to which was once guarded by the marine fortress of Svartholm. It was founded in 1745, with the name of Degerby, as a fortified outpost on the eastern border of Swedish-controlled territory, and renamed in 1752 after the wife of the Swedish king, Adolph-Frederik, who visited it in that year. The fortifications, after

Pori. Junnelius mansion (1895)
by A. Krook

Tampere. Art Museum, formerly
a granary (1838) by C. L. Engel

85

Kristiinankaupunki. Town hall (1858)

Loviisa. Town hall (1856) by G. T. Chiewitz

being surrendered to the Russians in 1808, were destroyed by the British during the Crimean War. Besides the town-hall, Loviisa contains a number of buildings of interest: the late seventeenth-century manor-house of Degerby (now a tourist centre), some narrow streets of eighteenth-century wooden houses, the municipal museum, built in 1755 as a residence for the commandant of the fortress, and a neo-Gothic church of 1865, also by Chiewitz. Nearby, on the road to Kotka, at Ruotsinpyhtää, are the eighteenth-century wooden buildings of a waterside ironworks, one of Finland's earliest examples of industrial building.

Kristiinankaupunki

Another town (see Raahe above) founded by Per Brahe in 1649. It surrounds a small bay opening on to the Gulf of Bothnia, and has a busy export harbour. The architect of the town-hall, built in 1858, is not recorded, but it could well be a product of the official office set up by C. L. Engel, and in any case illustrates the persistence into the second half of the nineteenth century of the restrained classical idiom that he established, through this office, all over Finland. Kristiinan-kaupunki has kept much of its traditional character, derived from the low wooden houses that still line its narrow streets—(see Chapter 7).

Pietarsaari. Town hall (1877) by
G. Wilenius: entrance porch

Vaasa. Town hall (1878) by
Magnus Isaeus

Pietarsaari (Swedish, Jakobstad)

This well laid out industrial town on the shore of the Gulf of Bothnia
was founded in 1652 by Ebba Brahe, the widow of Jacob de la
Gardie, after whom it is named. The town-hall is unusual in being
all of wood, unplastered, painted in two shades of buff. It was
designed by G. Wilenius and built in 1877 and is lavishly enriched
with the carpenters' ornament of the period, especially in the
entrance porch shown in the photograph. Pietarsaari is another
town which still possesses many streets of old-style wooden houses—
(see again Chapter 7). It also contains one of the most handsome
early nineteenth-century residences in the provinces: Malm House,
by A. F. Granstedt (1836–8).

Vaasa

The town-hall at Vaasa, facing one of the tree-planted squares laid
out by C. A. Setterberg (see under Old Vaasa, page 73), is a more
sophisticated example of the ornate civic buildings of the period
when the shipping trade, based on the Finnish ports along the Gulf
of Bothnia, brought considerable prosperity to the region. The
town-hall was designed in 1878 by a Swedish architect, Magnus
Isaeus. Vaasa became for a short time the capital of Finland during
the 1918 War of Independence.

Helsinki. House of the Nobility
(1861) by G. T. Chiewitz

Helsinki. University Students'
Union (1870) by Hampus
Dalström

Helsinki. The *Ateneum* (1887) by C. T. Höijer

Helsinki (Swedish, Helsingfors)

The House of the Nobility, by G. T. Chiewitz (1861), marks the introduction into the civic architecture of the capital of eclectic styles such as had long been fashionable elsewhere in Europe, replacing the hitherto unvaried neoclassical. It is an ambitious design in brick and stone, introducing traceried windows and other Gothic-flavoured details into a flat, symmetrical façade subdivided vertically and horizontally in Renaissance fashion. It stands north east of the Lutheran cathedral and contains an impressive stairway and a large assembly hall with beamed ceiling and panelled walls adorned with armorial bearings.

The University Students' Union, at the corner of Aleksanterinkatu in the heart of Helsinki, shows—in contrast to the building just illustrated—the persistence of the classical tradition. Designed by

Hampus Dalström in 1870, it has an unusually elaborate façade, but one treated with considerable refinement. It has an assembly hall now used as a theatre and a music-room with frescoes by Gallen-Kallela.

The *Ateneum* is a typical example of the work of Carl Theodor Höijer, the leading architect in the 1880s and 1890s. He was trained in Sweden and then became a pupil of Chiewitz in the latter's office at Turku. Höijer's richly modelled Renaissance façades enliven a number of Helsinki's central streets. The *Ateneum* (1887) is the Finnish national art gallery and faces the national theatre across the railway station square. The photograph shows its side elevation to Keskuskatu.

The Esplanade is the wide, tree-lined avenue, with a pedestrian

Helsinki. Office building,
Erottaja (1889-91) by C. T. Höijer

Helsinki. Commercial buildings,
North Esplanade (1888) by
K. A. Wrede

90

Helsinki. House of Estates (1891) by Gustav Nyström

park down its centre, which connects the centre of the city with the South Harbour and its market place. It has a variety of handsome buildings, including the characteristic late nineteenth-century commercial buildings here illustrated, with richly modelled Renaissance façades. They are at the western end of its northern frontage and were designed by K. A. Wrede in 1888.

Another, and very richly textured, example of C. T. Höijer's neo-Renaissance commercial buildings is in Erottaja, near the centre. It was designed in 1889–91 and is now occupied by the Government Forestry Board.

The House of Estates (1891) is a typical example of the work of Gustaf Nyström and shows how, in his hands, the neoclassical tradition was continued up to the end of the century with considerable vigour and assurance. The pediment above the Corinthian portico has bronze sculpture by E. I. Wikström (1903). The building stands to the north east of Senate Square, in Snellmaninkatu. In it, and its predecessor, the national diet (consisting of four estates—the nobility, the clergy, the burgesses and the peasants) met from 1863, when the liberal Emperor Alexander II summoned it for the first time since 1809, until 1906 when single-chamber government was instituted. The building now houses various scientific societies.

**Hamina. Reserve Officers'
Training School (1898)**

Hamina (Swedish, Fredrikshamn)

The main building of the Reserve Officers' Training School is another example of the continuation right up to the end of the century—the building is dated 1898—of the traditions and disciplines of the neoclassical era. The academy was built during the Russian regime for the training of Finnish cadets. The remarkably planned eighteenth-century fortress town of Hamina is described and shown from the air on page 72.

Tampere (Swedish, Tammerfors)

The municipal theatre (1912) is a late neoclassical building by Kauno S. Kallio, Greek in flavour but showing also traces of the *Art Nouveau* phase through which Finnish architecture had just been passing. It maintains at the same time the flatness of façade modelling that is characteristic of Finnish architecture of whatever era. The theatre faces on to Tampere's central square, alongside, but somewhat set back from, the church by Bassi shown on page 50.

Helsinki (Swedish, Helsingfors)

The Parliament building at Helsinki (1927–31) is Finland's most prominent example of the formalized neoclassical style that was developed in Sweden in the 1920s (eg Ivar Tengbom's Stockholm concert-hall) and much imitated elsewhere. It is a monumental composition in red granite, which loses some of its effect by standing in bleak isolation beside Mannerheimintie, one of Helsinki's main arteries, without being tied into its surroundings by supporting buildings or sympathetic landscaping. The architect was J. S. Sirén, winner (with his then partners, Borg and Åberg) of a competition held in 1924. It has a symmetrical plan with a high circular chamber in the centre.

**Tampere. Municipal Theatre
(1912) by S. Kallio**

Helsinki. Parliament Building
(1927-31) by J. S. Sirén

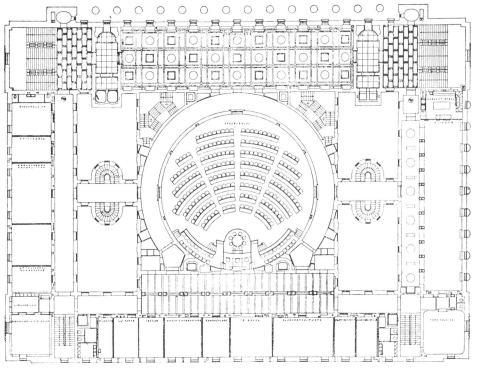

Main floor plan of Parliament
Building, Helsinki

7 Wooden Town Houses

For the connoisseur of vernacular styles of building Finnish towns are fascinating places, full of unrecorded treasures and unexpected variations on a common theme. They will not remain so for long because the inevitable process of modernization and rebuilding means that the streets of low wooden houses, of which all Finnish towns at one time wholly consisted, are being swept away, and it is these buildings, with their endless variety of treatment and ornament, that constitute the Finnish town vernacular.

Being built of wood, the domestic buildings—and to a great extent the commercial buildings also—were seldom more than one or two storeys high, though they were sometimes raised above the pavement on low stone basements. The combination of their consistent lowness, of their horizontal roof-lines and of the great width of the streets produces the distinctive look of the old-style Finnish town. In spite of the absence of height it is not a suburban look, since there is no scattering of buildings with space opening out between them, no sense of streets winding away into the country. Streets are continuously built up and enclose geometrically laid-out, truly urban, spaces. There is, nevertheless, a refreshing sense of breadth about the traditional Finnish townscape and of the sky dominating the scene, to which the yellow ochre, white and grey of the paintwork, and the flat façades—modulated, but only lightly, by fanciful carpenters' ornament—contributes an unusual mixture of austerity and idiosyncrasy.

These broad streets, as the introductory chapter of this book observes, have the functional purpose of preventing the spread of fire and of leaving space at the sides for banked-up snow. And the fire hazard is one of the reasons why this town vernacular has been disappearing during recent years. Other, equally obvious, reasons are the need for multi-storey buildings, for which wood construction is unsuitable, and the general tendency to congregate in towns. The result is that the Finnish town, which for centuries was no more than a modest trading and administrative centre at the service of a mainly rural population, has now become almost as much the typical environment of the people as it is in other European countries. In the thriving modern towns, with their substantial buildings, heavy traffic and energetic exploitation of advanced technology, the old wooden houses can no longer claim a place.

Few efforts have been made to keep them for yet another reason: they have not hitherto been taken seriously as architecture and have been identified with old-fashioned living—looked down upon as the opposite of progressive. Or this was so until three or four years ago. Since then, it is gratifying to be able to report, there has been something of a change of heart, especially in those smaller towns, such as the seaport towns on the Gulf of Bothnia, where wooden houses survive in great numbers and where there is not the same need as in the larger cities for multi-storey redevelopment. The sea, moreover, has long been retreating from these towns, since the land is rising at the rate of one metre every hundred years, so that new industrial and maritime development tends to take place at some distance from the old centre.

Towns such as these, in which many of the accompanying photographs were taken, are beginning to value their inheritance of old houses and the historic associations they evoke, and—often to the authorities' surprise—the occupants of the houses have been found to be sufficiently attached to them to prefer rehabilitation to total rebuilding. As a result, town plans that had involved the sweeping away of whole areas of old wooden houses have lately been replaced by new plans in which groups of such houses—sometimes comprising quite substantial residential quarters—are marked for preservation. Measures are being taken to rehabilitate decayed or inadequately equipped houses and to give individual house-owners financial help and expert advice so that they can do the same.

The Finnish Government, moreover, is backing this conservation campaign. By legislation enacted in 1977 it has designated thirteen towns for the receipt of special financial help in preserving their traditional wood architecture. This help will take the form of a subsidy enabling municipal authorities to grant loans at a very low rate of interest to owners modernizing their wooden houses. The loans will cover 60 per cent of the cost and will be repayable in five years. The modernization must be done under expert architectural guidance. On the passage of this legislation the wholesale destruction of the old wooden houses in these small towns was stopped.

Although in some cases the newly demarcated conservation areas stand apart from the busy centre of the town and there may seem to be a danger of their preservation separating them from the real life of the town—freezing them, as it were, in an unreal posture looking only to the past—this danger is not as real as one might imagine because, suitably modernized, the old wooden houses are surprisingly comfortable and their construction adequately resistant to Finland's testing winter climate, and they are much sought after.

Certain areas of a few of Finland's older towns contain streets of wooden houses of some antiquity, but most of the wooden houses with which this chapter is concerned are not in fact very old. The methods of building and the styles of finish and ornamentation have changed little over the years as houses have been built and rebuilt, and the bulk of such houses date from the closing decades of last century and the early years of this.

They are the work of local builders who presumably garnered ideas for their endlessly varied architectural embellishments from pattern-books and other illustrated publications. The embellishments take many forms: classical pilasters—often of eccentric proportions—window and door hoods, cornices—carved and bracketed—and fretted gables and barge-boards. They are naive and of course quite untutored as regards the correct use of the classical vocabulary from which—at several removes—they are derived. But they possess great individual charm, and sometimes (as several of the examples photographed herewith reveal) inventiveness to the point of fantasy. What is more important from the point of view of the towns as a whole, they give a most welcome consistency to the urban scene.

Such houses are invariably of either one or two storeys, mostly the former. In some regions, from about 1820 (that is, from soon after the beginning of Russian rule), two-storey houses were forbidden for a number of years because of the risk of fire. The mansard type of roof, permitting habitable top floors, was similarly forbidden, and for the same reason the original shingle-covered roofs gave way to other materials; shingle roofs are now altogether forbidden. Fires nevertheless continually occurred, but repeated rebuildings seldom brought about any change in the street pattern because the stone bases on which houses were erected survived the

fires, and it was easiest to build the new house on the old base.

The earliest form of wood construction was with walls of solid logs, exposed on the outside. By the seventeenth century it had become usual to cover the logs with boarding as an extra protection from the weather, the boarding being set vertically with small fillets over the joints. In the eighteenth century it was more usual to cover the logs, or the timber framing that had by now often replaced them, with horizontal boarding tongued and grooved, and later still one finds a mixture of vertical and horizontal boarding on the same façade. The construction and workmanship were of high quality, perhaps because much of the work, especially in the small towns on the Gulf of Bothnia where the old wooden houses survive most consistently, was done by the local shipwrights and ship's carpenters.

The houses were painted: at first red or yellow, which were earth colours, water-based, and later with oil-paints but still in a limited range of creams and buffs with an occasional contrasting dark green or blue. Door and window details, and such things as cornices, were often picked out in white. The houses were normally built right up to the line of the street, with ways through at intervals to yards and outbuildings behind.

Uusikaupunki (Swedish, Nystad)

This is a typical small town on the Gulf of Bothnia, shown here by an air view in which the wide streets, with evenly spaced low wooden houses, can clearly be seen. The town was founded by Gustavus Adolphus II in 1617 and is famous historically for the peace treaty between Sweden and Russia signed there in 1721. Besides its good harbour, it lives on its stone quarries from which come large quantities of granite. The church spire in the distance belongs to the Gothic Revival New Church (by G. T. Chiewitz), built in 1863.

Uusikaupunki. Air view of centre

Porvoo. Street in the old town

Porvoo (Swedish, Borgå)

The old part of the town, situated on the hill which it shares with the medieval church (see page 28) and the town hall (page 71), retains many of its wooden houses, some surviving from the eighteenth century, irregularly sited along winding lanes on the medieval pattern.

Raahe (Swedish, Brahestad)

A seaport town on the Gulf of Bothnia, Raahe was founded in 1649 by Per Brahe, twice governor-general of Finland, from whom its name is derived. It reached the height of its importance in the nineteenth century when it was one of the principal bases of the world-wide Finnish trade, especially the trade in vegetable tar for ship-building. Iron-built ships and the Crimean War together destroyed its prosperity and the town stagnated for a hundred years until a steel industry—the largest in Finland—was established there in the 1960s. The steelworks, however, are somewhat removed from the town so that, in spite of a good deal of modernization and replacement of the old wooden merchants' and seamen's houses, it has

retained its nineteenth-century scale and pattern.

Between the Pekkatori Square, in the centre of which is a statue of Per Brahe, and the waterfront (on which stands the old customs house shown on page 76) are several streets, laid out as a regular grid, of single-storey, wooden seamen's houses. Raahe is one of the thirteen Finnish towns (see page 94) to which government subsidies to help preserve their old wooden houses are to be given, and half of this area of seamen's houses is to be preserved as a unit. In this half, covering 25ha (61.5 acres), 200 old houses are left—about 70 per cent of the original total. Of these 50 per cent are still in good condition and another 40 per cent can easily be put in order. The remaining 10 per cent will have to be demolished and rebuilt. This will be done in harmony with the rest, and there will also be some infill to replace the houses that have gone. The houses are mostly very small, but the town authorities believe that they can be sufficiently enlarged while being modernized or, in some cases, adjoining houses can be merged into one.

Raahe. Street of seamen's houses

Raahe. House in the old
quarter

97

Pietarsaari. House in the old quarter

Pietarsaari (Swedish, Jakobstad)

This is another ancient industrial seaport town from which—as elsewhere on the Gulf of Bothnia—the sea has receded so that Pietarsaari's outport (Leppäluoto—Swedish, Alholmen), an important outlet for Finnish timber, is 4km (2½ miles) away to the north, and the old town retains much of its traditional character. It was founded in 1652 by Ebba Brahe, the widow of the famous Swedish military leader, Jakob de la Gardie, after whom she named it. It prospered, like Raahe, as one of the bases of Finnish sea-going trade and from the export of vegetable tar for ship-building—an important product all down this coast. But—again like Raahe—Pietarsaari lost its maritime importance after the Crimean War and the coming of iron-built ships.

However, it retained some of its prosperity, because, in 1762, a large tobacco factory—the first in Europe—had been established in the town. A residential quarter was built near the factory to house 1,500 of its workers, and this is almost intact, having survived a fire which destroyed much of the town in 1835. As at Raahe, a new town plan, which will preserve this quarter, was made in 1974 to replace one which would have swept it away. It has narrow streets, laid out in a grid pattern, of low wooden houses, some adorned with high-quality carpenters' ornament. These are being rehabilitated, together with the houses in the adjoining Harbour Street, leading from the old waterfront to the church (page 42). For other buildings at Pietarsaari, see pages 87 and 134.

Rauma

This is yet another seaport town on the Gulf of Bothnia (but further south, and therefore in the province of Satakunta, not Ostrobothnia) with a similar history to Raahe and Pietarsaari. During the last part of the nineteenth century it had the largest fleet of sailing-ships in Finland, chiefly engaged in Baltic and coastal trade. The older part of the town has narrow streets of wooden houses still preserving the medieval plan. Two views above include one of a house that has employed, as part of its stone base, one of the natural outcrops of rock that occur so frequently in the Finnish landscape. The later town, with quays facing the sea, was maintained on the same site when the sea retreated, because a canal was cut, linking the old town to its new port. This nineteenth-century town has regular streets of well-maintained wooden houses, many richly ornamented. Two photographs (right) from this area, which is near the market and the eighteenth-century town-hall (page 70), show a house, painted pink and grey, with a pilastered façade, designed in 1890 by the local architect, Augustus Helenius, and a detail of a typical nineteenth-century window. Rauma is also among the towns that are to receive the government conservation subsidy mentioned above, and has the advantage over some of the others that its streets of wooden houses are still part of the thriving central area.

(*top left*)
Rauma. Street in the old quarter

(*top right*)
Rauma. House in the old quarter, built on foundation of natural rock

(*second right*)
Rauma. Wooden house in the newer town (1890) by Augustus Helenius

(*bottom right*)
Rauma. Window detail from a house in the newer town

Turku. Surviving wooden houses

**Turku. Looking into yard
between terraces of houses**

Turku (Swedish, Åbo)

Although in the larger Finnish towns the streets of wooden houses are inevitably and rapidly disappearing, Turku still has a few. These are typical of the style that was once ubiquitous, with their pattern-book embellishment and their mixture of horizontal and vertical boarding. The larger house on the left has, unusually, a full-height, stone, lower storey. The other photograph from Turku is taken looking into the yard between two terraces of similar houses and shows the double porches from which each pair of houses is entered.

Tampere (Swedish, Tammerfors)

Again the use of both horizontal and vertical boarding is seen in two photographs of wooden houses surviving in Finland's second largest city. The second shows a more fanciful style applied to a gabled house with a plastered lower storey which exhibits an interesting consistency of treatment between it and the wooden superstructure.

Tampere. Wooden houses

Tampere. Gabled wooden house,
plastered below

Naantali. Ornamented houses in the main street

Naantali (Swedish, Nådendal)

More elaborate gables and a wealth of carpenters' ornament are shown in these houses in the main street of Naantali, a small coastal resort within reach of Turku (see also page 36).

Vaasa. Wooden house (*c* 1870)
in the Russian military area

Vaasa

One of Vaasa's handsome sequence of open spaces was originally the
parade ground for the Russian military forces and is surrounded on
three sides by low wooden buildings that served various military
purposes, all built around 1870. This example, in the centre of the
east side, with an ornamental porch, was the officers' club.

Kaskinen. Gabled house

Kaskinen

A nineteenth-century wooden house in the Ostrobothnian village of Kaskinen, south of Vaasa, with ornamental gables in a style characteristic of wood architecture and some unusual decoration over the windows.

Mariehamn, Åland Islands.
House balcony

Mariehamn

A house with an ornamental balcony in the chief town of the Åland
Islands.

Oulu. Salt warehouses by the old harbour

Oulu

A group of eighteenth-century salt warehouses facing the waterfront (and the site of the docks before the sea retreated) in this town on the Gulf of Bothnia which, in the nineteenth century, was one of the main commercial centres in Finland.

Porvoo (Swedish, Borgå)

Old wooden town buildings are by no means all residential or ecclesiastical. Storehouses and the like were also of wood, and many examples survive alongside the Finnish waterways. This range of storehouses on the waterfront at Porvoo shows a more primitive form of wood construction, with walls of solid logs either overlapping at the corners or finishing against corner posts. The church in the background is that illustrated on page 29.

Porvoo. Waterfront storehouses

8 The Rural Vernacular

While wood is rapidly being replaced in the towns by more lasting and less inflammable materials, in rural Finland it retains its predominance. As a result, ever since sawn timber superseded roughly squared logs, the construction of farmhouses, barns and other countryside buildings has remained basically unchanged except for their roofing materials—thatch and wood shingles are rarely now used—and except for minor modifications arising from the use of factory-made building components and the demand for improved space standards.

Countryside building today has its roots, therefore, in the traditional rural vernacular—a simple vernacular, wholly dependent on the limitations and potentialities of wood, which nevertheless has an important place in the historic architectural scene if only because, until well into this century, Finland was predominantly a country of farmers, foresters and fishermen; town life developed late, and the only popular architecture was that of the countryside and, to a far lesser degree, that of the small seaport and market towns whose wooden buildings were discussed in the last chapter. It is the purpose of this chapter briefly to examine and identify the range and character of this ancient rural vernacular.

Because of its functional origin, it has much in common with other wood-based vernaculars, especially those of Sweden and northern Russia; but there are also differences—not only between the latter countries and Finland, but between the various Finnish provinces—derived from different farming methods and social and cultural influences. The photographs on the following pages have been chosen to illustrate these. The farm buildings in the Ostrobothnian province are given a greater superficial resemblance to those in neighbouring Sweden by the practice of staining the timber a dark earth-red—'Falu red'—which was, however, introduced into Finland barely a hundred years ago and is far less common in the eastern parts of the country.

In all parts the same progress can be observed: from primitive log construction, with the logs overlapping at the corners, to log construction with corner posts and then on to increasingly sophisticated combinations of wood framing and boarding. Roofs progress similarly from birch-bark, thatch, or closely-laid poles to the more weather-proof wood shingles (introduced from Sweden in the middle of the nineteenth century), the last supplanted in recent times by less inflammable, industrially made materials. The bases of buildings and, in the case of dwelling-houses, their chimneys are of dry-laid stone or sometimes brick.

Wooden buildings burn and decay, or have to be replaced when farming methods improve; so the basically unchanging nature of the rural vernacular does not mean that quantities of old buildings are to be seen in the Finnish countryside. A number do survive in the less developed areas, especially Karelia, Savo and eastern Ostrobothnia, but a convenient way of studying both Finnish vernacular buildings and the variations in style and construction evolved in the different regions is by visiting the outdoor museum founded in 1909 on the island of Seurasaari in the western part of Helsinki harbour. Here old farm and village buildings from many parts of Finland have been brought together and re-erected. Similar collections on a smaller scale, illustrating only the local vernacular, have been made elsewhere in the country. A good example is at Isokyrö, a village to the east of Vaasa, where a whole complex of farm buildings—farmhouse, barns, stables and sleeping-quarters for the farmworkers, enclosing a gated yard, and the neighbouring smithy, windmill and smoke-sauna—have been preserved as a rural museum.

One final comment must be made about Finland's rural vernacular: it was one of the sources of inspiration at the outset of the National Romantic movement to which the next chapter is devoted. When Finnish artists and architects were moved in the 1890s to rediscover a separate Finnish cultural identity as a form of resistance to Russian political domination, they first expressed this urge in architectural terms by building traditional log houses—Akseli Gallen-Kallela, the leader of the movement, beside Lake Ruovesi, and Lars Sonck in the Åland Islands.

Ikaalinen

The most primitive form of log construction is exemplified in this boatshed, built to house the church boat belonging to the village of Ikaalinen, a small lake-side village in the south-western province of Satakunta. The shed is now in the outdoor museum at Seurasaari.

Uusimaa and Häme. Store sheds
from rural farms, now at
Seurasaari

In southern Finland, when the normal means of communication was still only by water, each village had one or more such boats in which, on Sundays, the whole population proceeded together to church, sometimes a number of kilometres away. After the church service it was the custom for the men of the different villages to compete with each other by racing their church boats on the lake. Church boats were still in use in the 1930s.

Uusimaa and Häme

Various farmsteads in these two southern provinces of Finland were the original locations of these typical storehouses, re-erected in a row at the outdoor museum at Seurasaari. Though still of primitive construction, they show the beginning of more sophisticated architectural treatment, with overhanging gable ends sheltering their doorways and, in one case—a storehouse from a farm near the village of Pusula—with a railed balcony reached by a ladder-like stair.

**Kristiinankaupunki. Country-style
storehouse**

Kristiinankaupunki

A country-style storehouse in this seaport town on the Gulf of
Bothnia. The type is a common one, found in western Finland as
early as the fifteenth century. Often the upper floor served as summer sleeping-quarters for the farmworkers.

Karelia

A grey log farmhouse typical of the far east of Finland. This
example, built about the middle of the nineteenth century, comes in

**Karelia. Log farmhouse
(mid nineteenth century) now at
Seurasaari**

fact from Suojärvi, in the part of Karelia ceded to Russia in 1944, from whence it had been moved to Seurasaari in 1939. One half of the two-storey building, shown in the photograph, has windowless storerooms on the ground floor, with the family living-rooms above. The other half has a cowshed on the ground floor with a hayloft above. This practice of housing people, crops and animals under one roof—although in effect in separate accommodation—is characteristic of Karelian farms. Only the sauna and the threshing-barn were independent structures, probably to guard against fire.

Säkylä. Farm buildings, now at Seurasaari

Säkylä

A contrast to the Karelian farm, with all its uses catered for under one roof, is this farm from the village of Säkylä in Satakunta, typical of western Finland. It is now at Seurasaari. The dwelling-house and the various barns, stables, storehouses, sauna etc, are separate buildings but enclose a fenced-in courtyard. In many places there were two courtyards, one for the people of the farm, the other for the animals. The picture shows a range of eighteenth-century barns and animal houses along one side of a courtyard.

Irjanne

The farm buildings shown above are mostly of exposed log construction. In this group of rural buildings in the village of Irjanne, between Pori and Rauma, in which large and small storehouses stand on either side of the church bell-tower, construction has been refined and the walls are faced with closely fitted vertical or horizontal boarding, with corner posts. The latter are painted white and

(this being western Finland) the boarding a dark earth-red. The larger storehouse may have been one of the barns that were built by the government in many villages for storing grain to be distributed in time of famine.

Närpiö

A similar form of construction is used for this very unusual group of rural buildings. They surround a green space in front of the church in this village between Vaasa and Kristiinankaupunki. The church served a large area and many of its parishioners had therefore to travel long distances from remote farmsteads. Each such family had one of these wooden huts where they could sleep the night when coming to church on Sundays and for weddings or funerals. They tethered their horses under the shelter of the hut's projecting eaves. The huts are the traditional red and white, with shingle roofs. There are still 150 of them; once there were over 200.

Närpiö. Church huts for parishioners from remote farmsteads

Irjanne. Village storehouses and bell-tower

Säkylä. Farmhouse (c 1820), now
at Seurasaari

Isokyrö. Farm building

Ostrobothnia. Typical two-storey farmhouse

Isokyrö

This is a farm building in the rich agricultural area east of Vaasa. It is part of the complex of farm buildings (see above) including dwellinghouse, stables, barns and windmill, which is now preserved as a rural museum. The building, a stable, occupies one corner of the semi-enclosed courtyard typical of Ostrobothnian farms.

Säkylä

This is the dwelling-house belonging to the group of farm buildings from this village, now at Seurasaari, of which some of the barns and animal houses were shown above. But the house is later—about 1820

or 1830—and has a more developed style and building technique as well as window surrounds that show Empire influence. It faces into a courtyard surrounded by farm buildings.

Ostrobothnia

In this province two-storey farmhouses became common in the nineteenth century. This is a typical example, standing in the flat countryside east of Vaasa. It has red boarded walls with white trim and window-surrounds ornamented in a style similar to those in many of the neighbouring seaport towns.

9 National Romanticism and Art Nouveau

In most European countries the later years of the nineteenth century saw efforts on the part of pioneer architects and designers to find ways of escape from the academic straitjacket and from what seemed to them the cultural meaninglessness of applied historical styles. These efforts took various forms: in England, through the Arts and Crafts Movement founded by William Morris, they placed a new emphasis on truth to materials, especially as practised by the medieval craftsman; on the Continent of Europe, through the *Art Nouveau* Movement, initiated in Belgium by Victor Horta and Henri van de Velde, and through the Secession Movement in Vienna, they fostered a consciously non-historical style of design and ornamentation, linear in character and influenced by new developments in art and a newly awakened interest in the Orient.

In Finland, equivalent efforts began with the revival of peasant styles of building, especially those of Karelia, Finland's eastern province, where many of the traditional crafts survived. This revival, though inspired by the same impulses as had inspired Morris and his associates in England, was also a product of the political situation in Finland and the sentiments engendered by it. A deeply felt need for a sense of national identity, fortified by the repressions of the Russian regime which at that time was increasingly denying Finland the large degree of autonomy that the country had theoretically possessed since 1809, and denying the people even the use of their native language, found expression in representations and reminders of Finland's roots in the past. The same urge towards a national identity found expression in the music of Sibelius and the paintings of Akseli Gallen-Kallela, but it was most clearly evident in architecture and the applied arts.

Since, however, this revival of nationalist sentiment coincided in time with upheavals in the arts that were taking place in Europe for quite different reasons, and since the results of these upheavals penetrated into Finland, there grew up that episode, unique in the history of European art, in which a backward look at national traditions was mingled with a forward-looking allegiance to the newest revolutionary art movements—an episode usually, but inadequately, labelled National Romanticism.

Its first clear manifestation—at least as far as Europe was concerned—was at the Paris Exhibition of 1900. The official policy was that Finland should be displayed abroad as Russian, but, after resistance to this and after much argument, a compromise was reached whereby the Finnish industrial exhibits were to be shown with the Russian, but for the arts Finland was to be allowed to design and erect her own pavilion. This pavilion caused a sensation, with its bizarre mixture of styles taken from the Finnish rural vernacular and from the various international *avant-garde* movements. The building was designed, following a competition, by a trio of newly qualified architects: Herman Gesellius (1874–1916), Armas Lindgren (1874–1929) and Eliel Saarinen (1873–1950). Inside, it had frescoes by Gallen-Kallela and furniture and handicrafts from the Iris Factory at Porvoo which had been established in 1897 by Count Louis Sparre.

Sparre (1863–1964) was an amateur of the arts who played an important role at this time. He was a Swedish nobleman, who had settled when young in Finland and spent nearly all the rest of his life there, marrying the sister of Marshal Mannerheim. His closest friend was Gallen-Kallela with whom he had been an art student in Paris. Sparre provided the essential link between the National Romantic Movement and the English Arts and Crafts Movement. He had visited England in 1896 and called on Charles Holme, proprietor of *The Studio*, at the Red House, Bexley Heath, Kent, the house Philip Webb had built for William Morris in 1859 and which Holme had recently bought.

The Red House had marked the launching of the Arts and Crafts Movement, which was still a force in the 1890s with *The Studio* as its chief supporter and disseminator, publishing the highly influential small houses, and the furniture and fabrics, of such English architects as Voysey, Baillie Scott and Ashbee. Sparre brought their notions and attitudes back to Finland, where they took root and blossomed, and he founded the Iris factory, following the example of Morris a generation before.

The English influence is clearly seen at Hvitträsk, a group of houses and studios which Gesellius, Lindgren and Saarinen built for their own use on the edge of a lake to the west of Helsinki in 1901–2, on the strength of their success at the Paris Exhibition. Except for a few Karelian details, these rambling, open-planned domestic buildings might have been designed by Baillie Scott and much of the furnishing by Charles Rennie Mackintosh—then the outstanding *Art Nouveau* designer, though more widely recognized as such on the Continent of Europe than in England or Scotland.

In 1897 Sparre made another journey, this time to Brussels, and there he made another fruitful contact which was destined to have a stronger influence on the arts and crafts of Finland—and indirectly on the architecture—than he can possibly have imagined at the time: with Alfred William Finch Finch. was half English and half Belgian, had been a *pointillist* painter and had been one of the founders, with van de Velde, of the group of artists who called themselves *Les Vingt*. It was he who later persuaded van de Velde to turn from the fine to the applied arts and thus eventually to acquire his key position in the development of modern European architecture. By the time Sparre met him, Finch had himself turned from painting to ceramics and Sparre was so impressed with his work that he invited Finch to Finland to start a ceramics department at his Iris factory.

Finch came and stayed. He taught for twenty-five years at the Central School of Applied Art in Helsinki and exerted a powerful influence on the course of Finnish design. He provided Finland with a continuing link both with the European *avant-garde* and with the English Arts and Crafts Movement, about which he wrote articles in *Ateneum*, the Finnish magazine launched by Wenzel Hagelstam in 1898.

Links between Finland and the rest of Europe were maintained by other Finnish artists and designers, especially by Gallen-Kallela who himself visited Germany and England, and the National Romantic Movement developed by them soon embraced all the arts. For example, an artists' colony that was established on Lake Tuusula, just north of Helsinki, had among its members Jean Sibelius, the composer, whose house in the colony was built for him by another of the rising young architects of the movement, Lars Sonck (1870–1956).

In 1889 and again in 1890 Louis Sparre and Gallen-Kallela had together toured Finnish Karelia seeking out examples of indigenous peasant culture, and in 1894 Gallen-Kallela and his wife built for themselves, deep in the forest beside Lake Ruovesi (between Tampere and Virrat), a studio-house modelled on the traditional Karelian log-house. They furnished it with peasant utensils and with textiles designed by Gallen-Kellela and inspired by traditional patterns. It was their home for the next ten years and they occupied it intermittently for another seventeen.

In the same year Lars Sonck built his first houses—in the Åland Islands—likewise using traditional log construction, and before long the highly significant, although short-lived, National Romantic Movement established itself more publicly through a number of prominent buildings designed by the same small group of architects and a few others, all of whom—unlike the preceding generation of architects which had been trained abroad—emerged from the Helsinki Polytechnic Institute. As we have seen, they were familiar with, and influenced by, the work of Voysey, Baillie Scott and Mackintosh in Britain, by H. H. Richardson in America and by the Vienna Secession and the Jugendstil Movements in Germany and the Netherlands. But their basic inspiration was still in Finland's urge to establish her own identity, and for this reason the emotions that moved them were felt in a wider circle than that of the practising architects and artists. Nearly all these prominent buildings were the outcome of competitions, which would not have been won by designs so loaded with national symbolism had there not been a wider circle predisposed to welcome them.

The first of these buildings was the National Museum at Helsinki, the competition for which was won in 1902 by Gesellius, Lindgren and Saarinen. It is a highly picturesque building, reflecting the multiple influences, local and overseas, that contributed to this National Romantic Movement. It was soon followed by other buildings, in Helsinki and elsewhere, by these and other architects, the most important of which are illustrated and described on the following pages. Meanwhile Gesellius, Lindgren and Saarinen had also designed a number of domestic buildings including (1901–3) an ambitious country-house for a wealthy businessman at Suur-Merijoki, near Viipuri, on whose vaulted interiors painters, sculptors and all kinds of craftsmen worked together. It was much admired as a total work of art but was destroyed in the fighting of 1941.

The climax of the National Romantic Movement came in 1904 when Gesellius, Lindgren and Saarinen won the competition for a new main railway station at Helsinki. But that was also the end, for the tide was turning. Their design followed the same romantic mode, but it was attacked by the leaders of a new generation who saw no future promise in reminiscence and nostalgia; notably by Gustaf Strengell—a critic whose writings are in many ways comparable with those of W. R. Lethaby in England—and the architect Sigurd Frosterus. They were in touch with still newer developments in Europe in which romanticism played no part. Frosterus, in fact, was a pupil of van de Velde, whose work by this time showed increasing awareness of the new technologies and was leading forward to the uncompromising modernism of the coming decades.

A propos the competition design for Helsinki station, Strengell wrote: 'A building is no longer a picturesque silhouette, a huge dead immobile mass; it is a living organism which fulfils a certain purpose,' and when the station was eventually built, to a revised design, made five years after the competition by Saarinen alone, it was a monument of a different character, with smooth rounded forms replacing the first design's roughness and spikiness and with giant stylized figures replacing the bits and pieces of vernacular ornament. Though the building is richly embellished, ornament takes second place to enclosure of space and expressiveness of structure.

Saarinen was thus moving in the direction of European rationalism, a development no doubt accelerated by a number of tours he made in these years, accompanied by his wife—the sister of Gesellius—whom he had married in 1904. In that year they travelled through Germany, England and Scotland, and in 1908 they toured Germany again and—very significantly—visited Josef Olbrich in Darmstadt and Peter Behrens in Berlin. From these years dates Saarinen's interest in urban design which was to play an important part in his subsequent career. In 1908, too, he won first prize in a competition for a Finnish parliament house, producing a symmetrical building with a central tower—plain but somewhat heavily monumental—which was never built for political reasons.

The later work of Lars Sonck became, like Saarinen's, more formal and less dependent on the freedom of the picturesque; witness his symmetrically composed bank building of 1908 in the Esplanade at Helsinki, his church in the Helsinki suburb of Kallio (1909–12) and his Helsinki Stock Exchange (1911). These, though still highly personal in style, are duller than his early buildings, having discarded that slight element of the grotesque which gave the latter their idiosyncratic character without acquiring, like the best of Saarinen's, the different kind of vigour derived from new building techniques.

A number of commercial buildings designed around this time, by Lindgren, Frosterus, Selim Lindqvist (1867–1939; an architect of a slightly older generation whose work had always been coloured by international rather than national influences, especially influences from Vienna, and who was the first to build, in 1906, with a steel frame), Jarl Eklund and others, helped to establish a respectable idiom for city buildings that combined a functional sobriety of form with a sparing but inventive use of ornament.

European modernism was slowly taking over. Strengell and Finch wrote articles in *Ateneum* further expounding the virtues of simplicity as embodied in the buildings of van de Velde and the rising German school, and Armas Lindgren, after the break-up of his partnership with Saarinen, travelled like the latter in Germany and also met Olbrich and Behrens and other pioneers of the functionalist creed. This was of major importance because he returned to become director of the Central School of Applied Art in Helsinki, and the gospel he preached there was neither romantic nor nationalist. The road was opened to the new movements described in the next chapter of this book.

The National Romantic Movement had lasted barely a dozen years, yet it not only produced the major buildings, with their amalgam of political and artistic significance, illustrated here, but through many minor buildings it endowed Helsinki, previously a neoclassical city, with a new architectural character, flavoured by, but standing somewhat aside from, European *Art Nouveau*. Although isolated buildings in similar styles can be seen in many countries, they do no more than give occasional piquancy to the orthodox street scene. In Finland, while the National Romantic Movement lasted, they *were* the orthodox—a new consciously devised vernacular. As a result Helsinki is richer in idiosyncratic *fin-de-siècle* architecture than any city except Barcelona (how close is the parallel between Finnish and Catalan nationalism?), and perhaps Brussels,

although Brussels has lately destroyed some of its outstanding examples.

This unique situation is to a great extent attributable to the widespread support given, especially by their fellow artists and intellectuals, to the pioneer efforts of the young romanticists, to the absence of any deeply entrenched public opinion to act as a brake on the acceptance of unfamiliar ideas, to the regular use of the competition system which threw open the greatest opportunities to emerging talent and to the simple circumstance that the men who became, during these years, the leading architects in the country were also the most thoughtful, open-minded and adventurous. The result was not only to make Finland a country of unusual interest today to students of the new architectural movements of the opening years of this century, but, by relieving Finnish architecture of the oppressive burden of preconceived styles and attitudes which the modern movement elsewhere had to struggle so persistently to shake off, to prepare the ground more thoroughly than in most other places for the eventual acceptance of the new architecture described in the next two chapters.

Hvitträsk

Here is the pioneer work of National Romanticism: a group of studios and dwellings designed from 1901 onwards for their joint use by Herman Gesellius, Armas Lindgren and Eliel Saarinen, on a wooded site rising steeply from the edge of a lake about 24km (15 miles) west of Helsinki. The first part to be built (1902), which the three young architects occupied temporarily while work on the remainder was going forward, consisted of a studio and workshop

Hvitträsk. Group of studios and dwellings (1902) by Gesellius, Lindgren and Saarinen

(later to be used as stables) with a large flat above. This was afterwards Gesellius's dwelling. It was simple in style, reminiscent of Karelian vernacular building. The remainder of the project is more original and sophisticated, and shows the influence of the new domestic architecture (itself based on a revived interest in vernacular building methods) that had lately emerged in Europe and particularly in England. It consists of a long range of buildings, characteristically irregular in outline, with the single-storey studio in the centre and a two-storey, L-shaped dwelling at either end, enclosing, with the first building, a rectangular courtyard. Materials were stone, partly plastered over, shingles and pantiles for the roofs.

The dwelling at the entrance end, occupied by Lindgren, had originally a square timber-faced tower surmounted by a tile-covered turret, but it was badly damaged in a fire and subsequently rebuilt to a smaller size and without the tower. The other dwelling, which has an additional storey in the roof, was occupied by Saarinen. On its far side the ground falls away steeply, and here the romantic siting of the buildings becomes evident. Overlooking the woods and the lake beyond, they are surrounded by terraces and loggias and half a century's growth of vegetation. These garden outworks are additions made over the years by Saarinen, for in the course of time Hvitträsk became solely his. Lindgren left the partnership in 1905 and Gessellius in 1907. Saarinen made alterations to adapt the whole complex of buildings to his taste and lived and worked there until he emigrated to America in 1923. Several assistants (who included Alvar Aalto) worked with him there and must have been influenced by Hvitträsk's style and originality.

The interiors preserve much inventive Arts and Crafts detail, including vast tile-faced fireplaces embellished with copper and iron

and furniture influenced by van de Velde, and there was a nursery (see photograph) resembling some of C. R. Mackintosh's interiors in Glasgow. The treatment of space and the subtle use of changes of level remarkably anticipate Frank Lloyd Wright's work as a pioneer of the open plan, although Saarinen cannot have known of this at the time of the design. Hvitträsk was half derelict in 1949, but was acquired by private owners who meticulously restored it. The only substantial change they made was to open up the main living-room of the original Saarinen dwelling into the studio-office which was previously entered only from the courtyard. The buildings were restored again in 1969-71, since then they have been publicly owned and open as a museum.

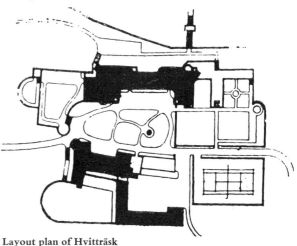

Layout plan of Hvitträsk

Hvitträsk. Nursery in the Saarinen dwelling

Helsinki (Swedish, Helsingfors)

The National Museum, by Gesellius, Lindgren and Saarinen (designed 1901; built 1905–12) was the outcome of a competition and was these three architects' first major building in the National Romantic style which they, together with Lars Sonck, were chiefly responsible for developing. Note in this early effort, as well as the picturesque irregularity of the composition, the not fully assimilated elements from Finnish medieval architecture such as the geometrical ornament in the gable. The rock-faced walls are of granite, the carved stonework of sandstone and the spire of brick roofed with copper.

The first residential building in Helsinki in which a mature version of the new romantic idiom was displayed was this block of flats in Fabianinkatu, also by Gesellius, Lindgren and Saarinen, built in 1901. It is dark grey in colour with powerful vertical lines, aroused great interest at the time and was followed by other tall blocks in similar style, by the same and by other architects, when areas of Helsinki like the Katajanokka peninsula (which had remained throughout the nineteenth century a poor quarter inhabited by fishermen and artisans) were built up soon afterwards.

Also dating from 1901 is Gesellius, Lindgren and Saarinen's Pohjola Insurance Building in Aleksanterinkatu—their first com-

Helsinki. National Museum (1905–12) by Gesellius, Lindgren and Saarinen

mercial building. It is in rock-faced stone, and its romantic outline is enhanced by decoration with a nationalist flavour like some of that on the museum. It has a fine staircase inside.

The National Theatre near the railway station, designed by Onni Tarjanne as early as 1902, shows the new romantic style combined with a consistent application of romanesque elements.

In 1904 Lars Sonck, the chief rival to Gesellius, Lindgren and Saarinen as a pioneer of National Romanticism, designed this bank interior with Valter Jung who was responsible for much of the decoration, notably the stained glass. This was the first of several interiors that introduced Sonck's unique and personal version of *Art Nouveau*. The banking hall was inserted into the eastern section, designed by Pehr Granstedt, of the early nineteenth-century Uschakoff Building at the north-east corner of the Esplanade (see page 77). Proportions are heavy and the elements massive, but the effect is one of spaciousness. The bank was completed in 1906 and restored in 1968 by Aarno Ruusuvuori. It now forms part of the city of Helsinki's public relations centre.

The Telephone Building (1905) in Korkeavuorenkatu, also by Lars Sonck, is typical of his most romantic phase. The skilfully

(*above left*)
Helsinki. Flats in Fabianinkatu
and (*right*) insurance building in
Aleksanterinkatu (both 1901) by
Gesellius, Lindgren and Saarinen

Helsinki. National Theatre (1902)
by Onni Tarjanne

Helsinki. Eira Hospital (1905) by Lars Sonck

Helsinki. Bank interior, Uschakoff Building (1904) by Lars Sonck

balanced façade (in spite of every group of windows being a different shape) is all in granite—rock-faced but relieved by the smooth door-surround and horizontal bands. In accordance with Finnish historical traditions, there is only the minimum of ornament, in the form of incised gometrical designs round the columns.

In his Eira hospital of 1905, Lars Sonck reduces his romantic style of composition with its irregular plan and roof-lines to a domestic scale appropriate to the building's situation in a new residential quarter of Helsinki (see page 124).

This residential quarter—Eira—of which a view is shown looking down a typical curving street, was laid out on English garden city principles in the southernmost part of Helsinki in 1907 by Bertel Jung, Armas Lindgren and Lars Sonck, with winding roads designed to be lined with individual villas. It was completely built up within a few years so that it presented—and still presents—a very consistent picture of the sophisticated taste in small house architecture of this time. The influence of English architects like Voysey and Baillie Scott can be clearly discerned, though the smooth white walls and simple geometrical forms have little in common with the nostalgic rusticity of materials and textures associated with much of these architects' work. Even more evident in the Eira villas is the influence of the Viennese *Jugend* style. Selim Lindqvist, who designed many of them, employed this style with assurance and sensibility.

Helsinki. Telephone Building
(1905) by Lars Sonck

**Helsinki. Eira residential quarter
(1907 onwards)**

The Mortgage bank building in the Esplanade (1908) and the Stock Exchange (1911), both again by Lars Sonck, are typical of his work at this time when he was replacing romantic picturesqueness by more formalized compositions, incorporating classical elements. His skill in juxtaposing masonry textures and in the placing of ornament is still there, but the result is somewhat stiff and lacking in vitality. In the Kallio Church, in a northern district of Helsinki (1909–12), this stricter formalism is even more evident. The church was the subject of a competition held in 1906.

The climax and the end of the Romantic Movement are represented by the successive designs for the railway station at Helsinki. It was the subject of a competition held in 1904 and won by Gesellius, Lindgren and Saarinen with a picturesque design resembling that of their National Museum. This was criticized by the younger generation of Finnish architects who were already being influenced by the more rational ideas developing elsewhere in Europe, and the executed design, made in 1907–14 by Saarinen

Helsinki. Mortgage Bank
building, Esplanade (1908) by
Lars Sonck

Helsinki. Stock Exchange (1911)
by Lars Sonck

Helsinki. Kallio church (1902–12) by Lars Sonck

(*right*)
Helsinki railway station: night view of entrance

(*below*)
Helsinki railway station (1907–14) by Eliel Saarinen

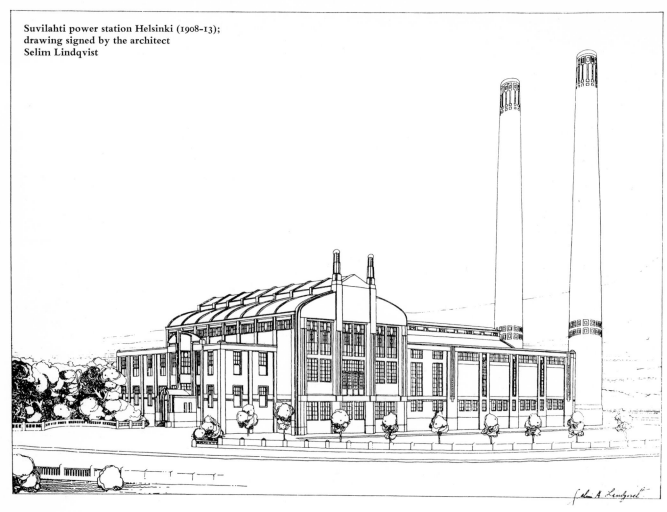

Suvilahti power station Helsinki (1908–13);
drawing signed by the architect
Selim Lindqvist

alone, has a quite different complexion. Modernity is no longer
overlaid by archaic affectations and picturesquely used references to
Finnish architectural history. In the plan, which is symmetrical
except for the clock-tower at the south-east corner and an administrative wing to the north-east, the main elements are the central
hall, with the main entrance under the great arch which forms one
end, and two secondary halls at right angles. All three have vaulted
roofs in reinforced concrete (used here for the first time in a major
public building in Finland), and these halls are clearly expressed in
the external massing; the whole building in fact, in spite of some
wilful stylizations, is a well articulated reflection of the internal
spaces and the structural means of enclosing them. The walls are
granite and the roofs copper. The pairs of giant sculptured figures
flanking the main entrance are by Emil Wikström.

The final illustration from Helsinki provides an interesting link
between the architecture influenced by the *Jugendstil* Movement in
Europe and that which marks the beginning of modernism and is
dealt with in the next chapter. It is the Suvilahti power station,
designed by Selim Lindqvist in 1908 and extended in 1913. The
power station, in spite of its traces of *Jugendstil* decoration, is
essentially a functional building, clearly expressing its reinforced
concrete construction. It provides Helsinki with a link with the more
original works of the Viennese Secession.

Tampere (Swedish, Tammerfors)

The cathedral at Tampere is Lars Sonck's most successful building
and his most important contribution to the National Romantic
style. It was the subject of a competition held in 1899 and was built
in 1902–7. Its historical reminiscences are well assimilated into a bold

Plan of Tampere cathedral

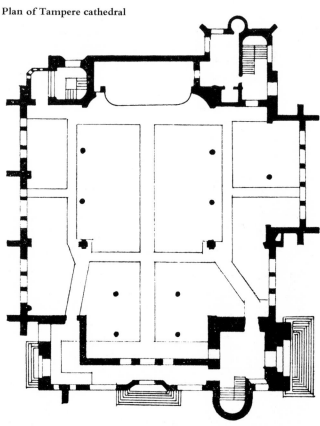

**Tampere cathedral (1902–7) by
Lars Sonck**

Tampere cathedral: west door and base of tower

and irregular but coherent composition. It has a square plan with a wide star-vaulted nave, narrow galleried aisles (widened on the south side to form a shallow transept) and the shallowest possible sanctuary, creating a spatial effect similar to that of the earlier Finnish cruciform churches in spite of its marked west-east axis. The latter is disguised externally by the typically romantic difference in size between the two western towers. Except around the west door, there is no embellishment outside save the pronounced textures of the materials—coursed rock-faced granite and red tiles. Inside, the style is orthodox *Art Nouveau*. The wall-paintings are by Hugo

Simberg except for the Resurrection over the altar, which is by Magnus Enckell. There is a marked contrast between this building and the stiffer, more classical, style that Sonck adopted soon after. During his last years he strongly criticized the style of the cathedral.

Like other Finnish cities, Tampere has prominently sited commercial buildings influenced by the Romantic Movement. An early and picturesque example: is the Palander Building in Tampere's main square. It was built in two stages; the first, by B. Federley, in 1901 and the second, by V. Heikkilä, in 1905.

130

Tampere cathedral: interior

Tampere. Palander Building
(1901-5) by B. Federley and
V. Heikkila

**Tampere fire station (1907) by
Vivi Lönn**

An *Art Nouveau* influenced building with great charm of detail is
the fire station at Tampere, designed in 1907 by Vivi Lönn, who
was one of the first women to practise architecture in Finland. She
specialized in schools and worked for a time in partnership with
Lindgren. She was born in 1872 and lived to be nearly a hundred.

Imatra

The picturesque Valtion (National) Hotel was built in 1903 alongside the rapids formed by the Vuoksi river cutting its way through
the steep rocky landscape to give the waters of Lake Saimaa—

**Imatra. Valtion (National) Hotel
(1903) by Usko Nyström**

Finland's largest lake—an outlet into Lake Ladoga. The rapids, which now lie almost on the Russian frontier, were a popular place of resort until a large power station was built (1921–9) across the river from the hotel, lessening both the force of the water and the charm of the scenery. The hotel, though much altered within, is an excellent early example of Finnish *Art Nouveau*, with picturesque elements that link it also to the National Romantic Movement. It was the principal work of its architect, Usko Nyström, who later became even more original and independent and was a teacher with unusually advanced ideas.

Pietarsaari. Water tower by
Lars Sonck

Pietarsaari. School (1912) by
Bertel Jung

Turku. Hamburger Börs Hotel (1903-8) by F. Strandell

Pietarsaari (Swedish, Jakobstad)

An unexpected work by Lars Sonck is this water-tower in the Ostrobothnian seaport town of Pietarsaari (see also page 98), with a definite *Art Nouveau* flavour. The house on the right of the photograph is by Alvar Aalto, but was intended by him to be faced in white stucco.

Near the quarter of old wooden houses in Pietarssari erected for the workers in the nearby tobacco factory (see page 98), and now the subject of a rehabilitation programme, stands this school by Bertel Jung, built in 1912, with a number of typical *Jugend* features including its battered lower walls and its picturesque outline.

Turku. Wooden house (1902) by F. Strandell

(right)
Rauma. House showing *Art Nouveau* influence

Turku (Swedish, Åbo)

Turku has a number of buildings in its central streets displaying Romantic and *Art Nouveau* influences. The best is the Hamburger Börs Hotel at the corner of the market place. In spite of recent alterations to the building, it retains many characteristic features of the Romantic period such as the asymmetrical composition of its façade and its eccentrically shaped windows. The hotel was designed by F. Strandell in 1903–8.

One of the surviving wooden houses near the centre of Turku, built in 1902 by the same architect, displays a number of vigorous *Art Nouveau* features.

Rauma

This more modest wooden house in this seaport town in Satakunta province again shows *Art Nouveau* influence in the shaping and embellishment of its front door and attached window.

10 The Beginnings of Modernism

After 1917 Finland was an independent nation and had no more need to make its architecture a symbol of its urge towards a national identity—cultural or linguistic. The National Romantic phase described in the preceding chapter had in any case been largely superseded, by the time World War I began, by simpler and more rational styles of design better suited to the needs of a modern urban civilization and reflecting the changes in aesthetic ideals then occurring in many parts of Europe. These included, as we have seen, changes arising from the revolution in domestic architecture that had taken place in England, from the *Art Nouveau* Movement as it had developed in Brussels, Paris and Vienna and from parallel developments in Germany.

At the same time the philosophy that united the separate architectural experiments being conducted in different parts of Europe and America, which were eventually to lead on to the international phase of modern architecture, was being more widely understood in Finland; the writings, that is to say, of Strengell, and the rationalist ideas that Frosterus had brought back from his association with van de Velde, were proving to be a more lasting influence than the novelties of style that had provided the first visible evidence of change; so the developments dealt with in the preceding chapter not only served the purpose of emancipating Finnish architecture from the academic sterility that would have stood in the way of the prompt adoption of modern architecture, but they laid the foundations of modern architecture itself. Two new factors that appeared during the years after World War I, which encouraged the building of a substantial structure on to these still somewhat tentative foundations, were a new sense of architecture's social responsibilities—resulting from the housing and similar problems Finland was faced with at the end of the war—and an increasing awareness of the implications of new building techniques.

At first, however, the architecture resulting from these more rational attitudes was relatively unexciting, and some of the best of it still harked back to the earlier romanticism; for example, the Käpylä housing in Helsinki (1920–5: architect, Martti Välikangas), a charming complex of low wooden dwellings laid out in English garden-suburb style. In general, the Finnish architecture of the 1920s, though plain, had the plainness of the neoclassical tradition rather than that of the structurally more expressive functionalism that was already a powerful movement on the Continent of Europe.

This movement took hold of Finland at the end of the 1920s, partly under the influence of the Swedish architect, Gunnar Asplund, himself previously a neoclassicist, who signalled his conversion to functionalism at the epoch-making Stockholm exhibition of 1930, but more particularly as a result of the clear-sightedness and the example of two Finnish architects, who were both working in Turku and who had become familiar by direct experience with the new ideas current in Europe. They were Erik Bryggman (1891–1955) and Alvar Aalto (1898–1976). Together they made the designs for an exhibition held in Turku in 1929 to celebrate the seven-hundredth anniversary of that town's foundation. In it, though the exhibition was a modest one, their new architectural allegiances were clearly made evident. Aalto, who had learnt from Frosterus and had therefore had direct access to the new ideas germinating in northern Europe, practised first in Jyväskylä where he designed a number of buildings of simplified form but still recognizably neoclassical in style. He moved in 1927 to Turku and almost at once showed evidence of the powerful contribution he was to make to Finnish—and before long to world—architecture.

In the same year he designed the *Turun Sanomat* newspaper building in Turku (built 1928–9) and won the competition for a public library at Viipuri (built, after a number of modifications, 1930–5). Both designs were structurally advanced and uncompromisingly modern. In 1929 he won the competition for a building of even greater impact: the tuberculosis sanatorium at Paimio (built 1929–33), with a design showing remarkable plastic invention as well as planning ability and structural enterprise. This and the Viipuri library (now in Russian territory and reconstructed after severe war damage) were Finland's first major contributions to the new international style of modern architecture.

In these two buildings also Aalto (now assisted by his wife Aino) first experimented with the bent plywood furniture that was later to be so closely associated with his name and was profoundly to influence furniture design all over the world. In several of their interiors, too, were to be seen foretastes of the very personal idiom, based especially on the use of wood, that he was to develop later; for example the undulating wood-strip ceiling in the lecture-room at Viipuri.

An architect who showed promise, before his early death, of becoming a third pioneer was Pauli Blomstedt (1900–35). He designed the Finnish Savings Bank at Kotka (1935), a hotel at Rovaniemi (completed 1936), a church at Kannonkoski (1938) and the very distinguished Aulanko Hotel (also 1938) in a park 4km (2½ miles) north of Hämeenlinna. The church and the Aulanko Hotel were completed after his death by Märta Blomstedt, in the case of the latter in collaboration with Matti Lampén. The hotel has been subsequently much altered.

Besides his most admired building, a cemetery chapel outside Turku (1939), Erik Bryggman, who stayed on in Turku after Aalto had moved to Helsinki, designed a number of other buildings there, including a hotel (1929) in a part of the town for which he also made the plan, a library (1935) for the Åbo Akademi—the Swedish-language university—and an insurance company's offices (1938). Other architects who designed noteworthy modern buildings in Finland during the same years were Hilding Ekelund (church at Töölö, Helsinki, 1929), O. Flodin and E. Seppälä (Tampere railway station, 1936), J. S. Sirén (the severe, plainly fenestrated office building of Lassila and Tikanoja, Helsinki, of 1935, which came surprisingly soon after his highly eclectic Parliament House), Lindegren and Jäntti (Olympic stadium, Helsinki, 1934–40) and Erkki Huttunen (church at Nakkila, 1937; industrial buildings at Oulu, 1938). Huttunen also made a number of designs for small wooden houses using standardized parts that interestingly anticipated the prefabricated house designs of twenty years after.

The work of these architects was sober, sincere and unassuming. The power and originality came from Alvar Aalto, who took the lead in the struggle to win acceptance in Finland for the principles of modern architecture that Gropius, Le Corbusier and the other participants in the *Congrès Internationaux d'Architecture Moderne* were spreading throughout Europe—congresses in which Aalto took an active part. In the 1930s it was his increasing authority that gave Finland its reputation as a country that had not only accepted the precepts and practices of modern architecture but was capable of making its own contribution to the process of bringing it to maturity. This was dramatically demonstrated abroad by his two Finnish pavilions—for the Paris exhibition of 1937 and the New York world fair of 1939. Though outside the scope of this book, these pavilions are too significant to ignore if only because they illustrate yet again the close connection that has always existed between the evolution of Finnish architecture and Finland's urge to establish national identity.

In these years Alvar Aalto, as a hero figure, stood virtually alone. Lars Sonck was no longer very active, nor had his work grown away —as Saarinen's had—from his earlier eclectic allegiances; and Saarinen himself, whose main enterprise after 1917 had been to prepare designs—never executed—for a monumental museum of Finnish folklore, commemorating the country's independence and set in a characteristic landscape of lakes and forests, had emigrated to America in 1923.

Helsinki (Swedish, Helsingfors)

The Stockmann department store in the middle of Helsinki, by Sigurd Frosterus, was the outcome of a competition held in 1916, but only a small part of it was built then, the remainder being completed between 1924 and 1930. It clearly shows, in the logical

Helsinki. Stockmann store (1924–30) by S. Frosterus

Helsinki. Housing at Käpylä
(1920–5) by M. Välikangas

Helsinki. Workers' housing (1928)
by Lindgren and Liljeqvist

expression of its frame construction, its affinity with the more advanced of the Dutch, German and other European work of the time, exemplifying principles that Frosterus had consistently followed while others of the pioneer generation of Finnish architects were liberating themselves from nineteenth-century academicism by the more roundabout route of nostalgic romanticism and formalism of various kinds. The building is of red brick externally, with a copper roof. Inside there is a column-free central hall rising the full height of the building and top lit, which the upper floors overlook from galleries.

Workers' housing was one of the themes of the 1920s, in Finland as elsewhere in Europe, and the civic authorities built several schemes in Helsinki that were comparable both socially and architecturally with the best in Germany, Holland and Austria. Left is one of the examples that still provides an agreeable environment: designed by Armas Lindgren and Bertel Liljeqvist in 1917: completed in 1928.

In contrast to it, the Käpylä housing, designed by Martti Välikangas to a plan devised by B. Brunila and Otto-I. Meurman and others and built 1920–5, clings to the English garden city principle (though with a rectangular grid layout) and to an architectural style based on the Finnish tradition of building in wood. Nevertheless it achieved excellent spatial and environmental standards and was at the same time an early example of the use of standardized structural elements. It has recently been thoroughly renovated, and Käpylä, in its setting of well grown trees and gardens, has become a highly desirable residential quarter occupied by the professional classes and the intelligentsia rather than the workmen for whom it was originally built.

Jyväskylä. Working men's club
(1925) by Alvar Aalto

Jyväskylä

This is a typical example of Alvar Aalto's early work in his home
town in which he first practised: a working-men's club, built in
1925. The accommodation inside—a meeting-room above and a
restaurant below—is clearly expressed on the exterior, and the
sharply punctuated wall-surfaces echo some international fashions
of the 1920s. These reveal an urge towards modernism which the
superficial neoclassical treatment goes some way to disguise.

Turku (Swedish, Åbo)

This is the first building in which Aalto fully committed himself to
the international modern movement. Built in 1928-9 for the
Turun Sanomat newspaper, it was Aalto's first substantial commission, and in it he showed his appreciation of the aesthetic
potentialities of new methods of construction and adopted such
devices, characteristic of the time, as the strip window. The picture
shows the machine-hall housing the printing presses. This and the
paper storage hall have their ceilings supported by tapering and
mushroom-headed reinforced concrete columns respectively, the
former especially—as vigorous as tree-trunks—showing great
subtlety of modelling. One of Aalto's favourite devices, the cylindrical roof-light, also makes its first appearance in this building.

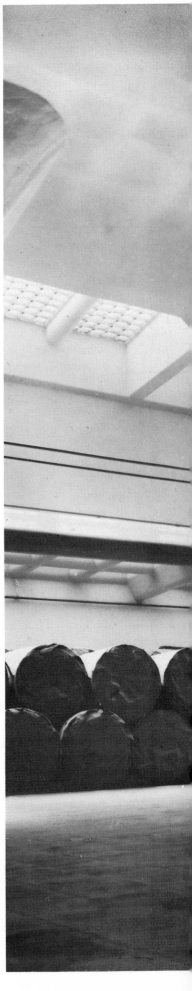

Turku. *Sanomat* newspaper building (1929) by Alvar Aalto: the
machine hall

Paimio

Alvar Aalto's tuberculosis sanatorium, now a general hospital, remotely situated in thick forest about 29km (18 miles) east of Turku, is the building that first put Finland on the modern architectural map. Aalto's winning competition design was made in 1929 and the sanatorium was built in 1929–33. It is informally planned, each department occupying a separate wing and the wings radiating from the centre at different angles, determined by the direction of sunlight and view. The reinforced concrete frame construction is fully exposed and fully exploited aesthetically: taut and muscular, yet gracefully modulated. The infill walls are brick, covered with plaster. In the second photograph, which is taken looking east into the three-sided entrance court, the patients' wing is on the right, rising above the tree tops and turning its wide windows and balconies (which are on the far side) towards the low northern sun. The open balconies have recently been glazed in.

Paimio sanatorium (1929–33) by Alvar Aalto: looking west

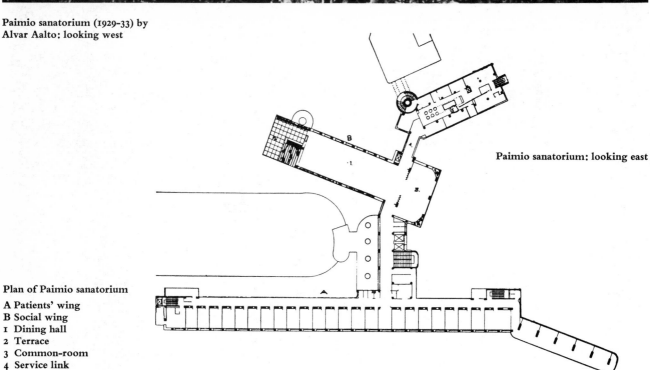

Paimio sanatorium: looking east

Plan of Paimio sanatorium

A Patients' wing
B Social wing
1 Dining hall
2 Terrace
3 Common-room
4 Service link

Helsinki. Insurance company offices in Kaisaniemenkatu (1930) by O. Kallio

Kotka. Bank (1935) by Pauli Blomstedt

Helsinki (Swedish, Helsingfors)

This insurance company building in Kaisaniemenkatu, designed by Oiva Kallio in 1930, was one of the earliest Finnish buildings to deploy such favourite devices of international modernism as the continuous horizontal window, but the difference of scale and treatment between the upper and lower parts shows that the new idiom has not yet been fully assimilated. In the evolution of modern architecture in Helsinki this building is, nevertheless, a landmark.

Kotka

This bank building at Kotka, by Pauli Blomstedt (1935), shows much more assured handling of the new international idiom, and a consistency of treatment indicating that its principles were fully understood.

Nakkila

One of the first modern churches in Finland was this country church in Satakunta, south east of Pori, by Erkki Huttunen, built in 1937. It has a rectangular nave, seating one thousand, a side-lit sanctuary with a semi-circular apse, a western tower and a crypt. The nave has a corrugated ceiling of wood boarding. Alongside the church is a sensitively designed low range of buildings, forming a parish centre and added by Juha Leiviskä in 1970.

Helsinki (Swedish, Helsingfors)

The Olympic stadium, by Yrjö Lindegren and Toivo Jäntti, is in a park at the northern end of Mannerheimintie. It was designed in 1934 for the Olympic Games planned to take place at Helsinki in 1940 but postponed because of the war. The building was extended, with its seating capacity increased to 70,000, in time for the Olympic Games of 1952.

The warehouses on Katajanokka, the built-up promontory separating the South from the North Harbour, were designed in 1937 by the city architect, Gunnar Taucher. They illustrate the straightforward, somewhat Germanic, functional style that was by this time coming to be accepted in official, as well as in the more advanced private, architectural circles.

(top left)
**Nakkila church (1937) by
E. Huttunen**

(top right)
**Helsinki. Olympic stadium
(1934-52) by Lindgren and Jäntti**

(left)
**Helsinki. Warehouses on
Katajanokka (1937) by Gunnar
Taucher**

Sunila

On the coast of the Gulf of Finland, near the industrial and timber exporting town of Kotka, is the large cellulose (wood-pulp) factory of Sunila, designed together with an employees' housing estate by Alvar Aalto (1936–9) and later extended by him (1951–4). It is on the steep edge of an arm of the sea, so that sea-going ships can berth close in. The uneven rock-strewn site, instead of being blasted flat, has been dramatically exploited to allow the successive industrial processes to take place on descending levels, finishing at the quayside. A conveyor (on the left in the picture) takes the raw timber—a whole year's supply of logs, floated down by water or brought through the lakes by ship—to the highest point where the production sequence begin. Production buildings are brick; service and warehouse buildings white concrete.

The Sunila housing estate, which accommodates a thousand people, is sited inland from the factory and consists of paralle blocks of dwellings along the southern slopes of an undulating rocky site, with forest occupying the northern slopes and the access roads in the valleys between. In most of the blocks the upper floors are set back, providing open terraces in front of their windows. The steep slope allows the middle storey to be entered at ground level from the rear.

Sunila was the first important example of the patronage of modern architecture by Finnish industry; until then nearly all the modern architects' opportunities had been gained by winning competitions. Aalto was called in to design the Sunila plant and housing by the industrialist Harry Gullichsen, for whom and his wife Aalto built the house at Noormarkku illustrated next. The Gullichsens, with Alvar and Aino Aalto, also founded, in 1935, the Artek company which manufactures Aalto's furniture.

Sunila. Cellulose factory (1936–9) by Alvar Aalto

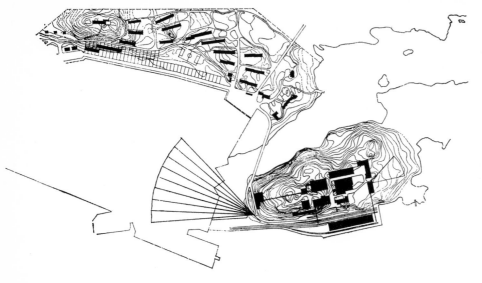

Layout plan of Sunila (housing opposite, above right)

Sunila housing (1936-9) by Alvar Aalto

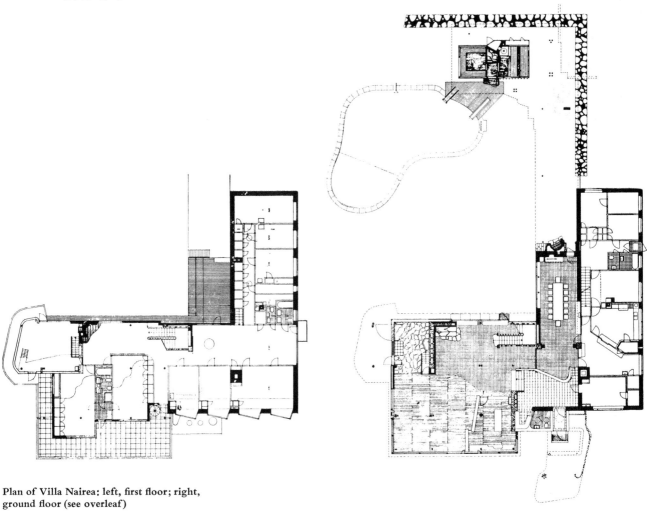

Plan of Villa Nairea: left, first floor; right,
ground floor (see overleaf)

**Noormarkku. Villa Mairea
(1938–9) by Alvar Aalto**

Noormarkku

This country house, the Villa Mairea, by Alvar Aalto and his wife
Aino (1938–9), is near the small village of Noormarkku, not far
inland from Pori. It occupies a hilltop site in the well forested park
belonging to the Ahlström family (see page 67). Mrs Maire Gullichsen, for whom the house was built, is a member of that family, and
it was her husband, Harry Gullichsen, who commissioned the
Sunila cellulose factory and housing (see page 148).

The house is L-shaped, with an extension in the form of a terrace
backed by a stone wall partly enclosing, with the house, a garden
court. A large part of the ground floor forms one space which can be
subdivided by movable partitions. This has a steel frame. Walls are
of brick, plastered. In many of the wood finishes Aalto experimented with the techniques he was to develop in his later buildings:

wood strips on walls and ceilings, close-set wooden rods serving as screens and so on. He had made similar experiments, though on a less ambitious scale, in his own house in the Helsinki suburb of Munkkiniemi, designed two years before.

Turku. Resurrection Chapel (1939-41) by Erik Bryggman

Turku (Swedish, Åbo)

The Resurrection Chapel in a cemetery on the south-eastern outskirts of the city of Turku is Erik Bryggman's most notable work, designed in 1939 and finished in 1941. It has a concrete frame and brick walls and an asymmetrical plan, with an aisle along only one side of the nave. The side wall within the aisle is wholly of glass, giving a view into foliage and trees.

11 Modern Architecture after 1945

When building began again after World War II, Alvar Aalto was the established hero figure of Finnish architecture and the one link between it and the international architectural scene of which he and his influence were increasingly part. His first important post-war building, the civic group at Säynätsalo, exemplifies the qualities for which he was by now widely admired and which determined the nature of his own very personal contribution to the rapidly maturing international idiom. It was the outcome of a competition held in 1949. Before then, after the end of the war in Finland, Aalto had been much in America, teaching at the Massachusetts Institute of Technology and designing a dormitory building there (1947–8). He returned urgently to Finland in October 1948 on learning of his wife's illness. Aino Aalto died in January 1949.

Säynätsalo (see page 154), as a conception, is original and inimitable. It was built at a time when architects were finding the puritanism of the early days of modern architecture, and its dependence on rectilinear forms and a machine aesthetic, cramping instead of inspiring; and as they faced the problem of fighting their way out of the narrow channels into which they had allowed it to lead them, they were encouraged to find that Aalto was already in possession of the wider, freer territory they were struggling towards. He had reached it by some route of his own, discovered intuitively, and, what is more, had escaped in doing so the occasional affectation and obsession with his own solutions that had limited the influence of Frank Lloyd Wright, an older architect of similarly heroic stature whose work had something in common with Aalto's in that its basis was a sense of architecture's organic wholeness.

Wright was a great man as well as a fierce opponent of the worship of technology, but obstinate as a mule and with as little chance of progeny. Aalto, on the other hand, was the prime exemplar of the open mind, and bore, in Finland, numerous progeny. These are, however, far from being direct disciples, let alone imitators. His influence can be seen in the work of many other Finnish architects, but they have developed in their own way. What they have in common with Aalto is an ability to use modern techniques adventurously, idiosyncratically and at the same time humanly, and to reproduce in their work the geometrical vigour and direct relationship between form and materials indigenous to Finnish architecture throughout its history.

In spite of its emphasis on the organic, modern Finnish architecture is not anti-scientific; witness Aalto's inventive use of plywood in the design of furniture—so scientifically exploited as to make it virtually a new material. Wood is the material with which his most personal designs are especially associated, and this again is wholly consistent with the way Finland and its landscape were with him and within him whatever he did—a fact that perhaps explains the slight lessening in assurance observable in the buildings he designed in countries other than Finland.

Birch and pine forests not only clothe Finland's primeval landscape, but are the source of the country's industries and the basis of its economy, and in the same way that Saarinen and his associates, when they first broke away from the sterile academic rules and preconceptions at the end of the nineteenth century, sought their inspiration in the log buildings of the Karelian countryside and the richly decorative patterns of the shingled roofs of medieval churches, so virility and virtuosity in the use of wood have become an instinctive and fruitful resource of most of the modern Finnish architects. Aalto's own handling of it, though original, was never eccentric; it had a quality of inevitability derived from his craftsman-like pleasure in perfecting the design of a building component in relation to the job it had to do, at the same time as he engineered its contribution to a coherent whole. His solutions to a design problem, however romantic they may seem, were the outcome of a strictly functional process of analysis.

The critic's inevitable insistence on the organic nature of Finnish architecture in general and Aalto's in particular, and on the inspiration it derives from Finland's testing climate, primitive topography and limited material resources, must not, however, lead him to classify it as regional in any provincial or chauvinistic sense. Nor must he lay too much emphasis on its roots in the soil of Finland. From these may be derived some of the qualities that mark it as recognizably Finnish, but its essential qualities are independent of local allegiances. Finnish architects are without sentimentality; though in certain ways regionally inspired, they are fully involved in the scientifically orientated international world of architecture.

A somewhat different kind of influence that is important in Finland—more so perhaps than anywhere else—as this book's account of the development over the centuries of a separate Finnish architecture has had repeatedly to point out—is the stubborn Finnish people's consciousness of their long drawn out struggle to assert and maintain their independence. This cannot be divorced from the nature of the architecture they create. In the case of Aalto, the successive stages of his career coincided exactly with the successive struggles and upheavals that have dominated recent Finnish history. He was born (in 1898) at the time of the strictest repression by Imperial Russia and of growing public restiveness because of it; he was a child during the first stirrings of revolution; national independence in 1917 saw the start of his architectural endeavours, and he grew to maturity as an architect just as Finland emerged from the ordeals—emotional as well as material—of World War II.

Finland had lost to Russia the wealthy eastern province of Karelia, which had not only resulted in severe economic difficulties, but had brought half a million refugees trekking into the remaining areas of the country, a number amounting at the time to 12 per cent of the whole population. This created urgent planning and resettlement problems. Between 1944 and 1955 Aalto—like Saarinen at a similar stage in his career, after the previous war—became for a time as much a townplanner as an architect, working on plans for expanded industrial settlements at Rovaniemi and elsewhere. In addition there were severe housing problems over and above those that inevitably follow a destructive war.

Throughout the 1940s Finland's architectural energies were concentrated on dealing with this and similar problems. In 1949 a national building-loan department (*Arava*) was set up to help in overcoming the housing shortage. Its work was not always architecturally distinguished and Finnish industrial development was not yet such that it could usefully exploit systematized building techniques, but the experience it offered kept the new generation of Finnish architects well in touch with social realities. Not until the 1950s, however, was the pre-war creativeness of Finnish architecture recaptured, a process assisted perhaps by somewhat less stringent economic conditions—the 1950s were years of intensive industrial growth and in particular of the development of hydro-electric resources—and it was assisted also by Finland's renewal of contacts with the rest of Europe and America. Finland continued, as it had done in the past, to look to the West culturally, though now compelled to look to the East rather more than to the West economically.

The post-war generation of Finnish architects was dominated at first by those who had been Aalto's pupils. Later, when one of his pupils of the 1930s, Viljo Rewell (1910–64), had established himself as perhaps the second most influential architect in Finland, it was his office that became the nursery of the growing and rapidly maturing number of able modern architects. Rewell was more of a rationalist and less of a romantic than Aalto, if only in the sense that his best buildings are more rectilinear and less dependent on unexpected sculptural invention; also less an expression of one man's personality. After the 1950s, although Aalto was admired and looked up to, there was something of a move away from his highly idiosyncratic answers to day-to-day architectural problems—even a reaction against the very fertility of his invention. This was perhaps inevitable, not only because Finnish architecture had to show that it was more than one man thick, but because the allegiances of the next generation of architects increasingly became merged with those of their colleagues overseas and involved with the latter's changing aspirations and priorities. Other names besides Aalto's established themselves, if not as household words, at least among those knowledgeable about architecture: the names, for example, of Ervi, the

Sirens, Pietilä, Kråkström and Penttilä, and more typical of the Finnish architecture of the 1960s and 1970s is the cool, precise, industrially orientated work of men like Aarno Ruusuvuori; work that derived—to look for a precedent among Aalto's contemporaries—less from him than from Aulis Blomstedt, a professor with widespread influence, as well as a practitioner. Aalto continued to win competitions, but he also worked much abroad and in Finland he became a somewhat isolated figure. It gave great pleasure to his admirers that in his last important building—the Finlandia Hall in Helsinki (page 164)—he proved that he had far from lost his mastery.

One final thing must be said about this great man—and it is something no Finnish architect, however divergent his allegiances, forgets—how much the profession as a whole owes to Aalto. In spite of the talent and energy shown by Finnish architects after the war, their increasingly sophisticated style of design did not establish itself without a struggle. Aalto was in the forefront of that struggle. The revolt against the academies of forty years before had prepared the ground, and Aalto's increasing international prestige was a powerful weapon, but full public support and intelligent patronage had to be painstakingly worked for. Aalto himself was given no opportunity to design a building in Helsinki, the capital (apart from his own pre-war house in the surburb of Munkkiniemi) until 1952—when he was fifty-four—and even this was the result of victory in a competition.

Since then public support has grown, and in Finland architecture is now—along with forestry—a profession with special prestige attached to it. This provides part of the answer to the question that is so often asked about modern Finnish architecture: how is it that a small, geographically remote nation, with limited resources and a relatively brief cultural history, has managed to become one of the leading nations of the world, to which the architects of other nations look up and to whose buildings they make respectful pilgrimage?

There are other answers too, and one can only think that the explanation of this phenomenon is that it is the cumulative result of several factors, which can perhaps be enumerated as follows. First there is, as already indicated, the influence and international reputation of Alvar Aalto, who still represents Finnish architecture to many in spite of the fact that in more recent years the range of architectural activities in Finland, and the variety of the talent available, have removed architecture far beyond the capacity of a single genius to determine. Secondly there is the prestige, already mentioned, accorded to architecture as a social as well as an aesthetic undertaking, and the attention given to it in the press. Thirdly, and closely allied to this, there is the prevalence of the competition system—nearly every major new building is the subject of a competition—which offers big chances to the architecturally still uncorrupted. The results of competitions, again, are fully reported and discussed in the press.

Fourthly, there is the *youth* of the country: when Finland became independent in 1917 more than one-third of the three million population was under fifteen—only one-seventh, incidentally, were town dwellers, but there are many more now. Fifthly, there is the very rapidity of the post-war process of industrialization, which has transformed Finland in a short time from one of the least industrialized countries in Europe and has given a sharp impetus to the evolution of new technical means and resources. Sixthly, there is the discipline imposed and the challenge presented by severe climatic conditions—Finland being, as I observed in the introductory chapter of this book, a land in which the rocks lie very near the surface: a statement that can be understood in more senses than one. And seventhly, there is the intense consciousness, again already referred to, of national identity, which naturally finds expression in architecture.

Although Finnish architecture has changed in the last twenty years, as much as anything else as a result of economic and social pressures, it remains true that the quality achieved is consistently good. This can to some extent be attributed to the status given to the art of architecture. Such a high status creates a confidence in the air; when a profession knows what is expected of it, that very expectation keeps aspirations, and the resultant standards, high. Even the run-of-the-mill work, such as the housing put up by developers and contractors with only the minimum of professional advice, though sometimes boring, is nearly always respectable; the faults in the environment such housing helps to create are not architectural ones, but result from the increasingly uncontrolled urban sprawl. It is not too much to claim that there are far fewer ugly new buildings in Finland than in other countries. As a result, architectural blunders stand out the more prominently, like the wantonly obtrusive oil-company headquarters which dominates the skyline between Helsinki and Otaniemi and which should not have been allowed. That one feels this so strongly is a tribute to the high quality of design one has come to expect in Finland—and nearly always finds.

And there is more to it than high quality according to international standards. In appraising Finnish architecture, we find ourselves returning again to its special genius for resolving the conflicts that bewilder and frustrate the architects of nearly every other nation. The modern architect inhabits a world of conflict. In every aspect of his profession he is drawn in two opposite directions. He has to discover how to use the new industrialized techniques and yet to evoke human responses; he has also to discover how to combine the international nature of modern architecture—founded on the conception that science knows no political boundaries—with its need to respond to local conditions and cultures. The achievement of the best of the modern Finnish architecture is that it manages to be scientific without being inhuman, regional without being provincial and individual without being whimsical or egocentric.

Säynätsalo

This group of civic buildings in central Finland, just south of Jyväskylä (Aalto's home town) and near where he had his summer cottage at Muuratsalo, was built in 1950–2 following a competition held in 1949, and serves a one-industry town founded by the Enzo-Gutzeit wood-products company (see page 157). It deserves pride of place in this chapter as Aalto's first post-war building and the most personal of all his buildings. It is intimate and idiosyncratic, with an unusual layout directly responsive to the *genius loci*. The various buildings forming the group—municipal offices, council chamber, library and officials' residences—are planned round a courtyard which is artificially raised above the surrounding wooded countryside by using the material excavated for the buildings' foundations. Gaps between the buildings allow access to the courtyard, from which all the buildings are entered, up flights of steps, and also allow views towards distant lakes and the penetration of the low northern sun. Materials are dark red brick, wood and copper, and the abruptly varied roof shapes, seen through closely planted trees, cause the whole group to be absorbed into the rugged landscape and to appear as a romantic intensification of the scene in which it is set down.

Säynätsalo. Civic buildings (1950–2) by Alvar Aalto; steps up to courtyard with council chamber beyond

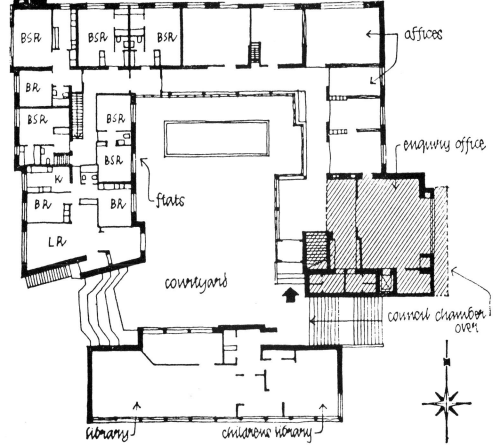

offices

enquiry office

flats

courtyard

council chamber over

library   childrens library

Plan of Säynätsalo civic
buildings

Helsinki. Rautatalo office
building (1954) by Alvar Aalto

Helsinki (Swedish, Helsingfors)

The Rautatalo (Steel Federation) office building in Keskuskatu, one
of the city's main shopping streets, was Aalto's first building in the
capital except for his own small house in the suburbs. It was completed in 1954 after a competition in 1952. The street façade, with
an unusual window layout which does not in fact reflect the floor
levels within, is framed in bronze. There are shops at street level, and
between them steps lead up to a high covered court housing a café—
an admirable answer to the problems of the severe winter climate.
The court is lined with travertine and surrounded by galleries from
which the office floors are reached.

The National Pensions Institute, by Aalto (competition 1948;
completed 1956), occupies a restricted triangular site in the northern
part of the city. In it Aalto reintroduced red brick for modern
Finnish town architecture. The brick buildings, copper-trimmed,
step up the slope and enclose a raised courtyard. The canteen, shown

in the interior photograph and in the exterior, (page 158), exemplifies Aalto's decorative inventiveness; note the metal ceiling panels containing heating units and the walls lined with rounded ceramic tiles —invented by Aalto for this occasion and used by him in several buildings subsequently.

The so-called 'House of Culture' (Alvar Aalto, 1958), is a meeting-hall for the Communist Party which is also situated in the northern part of the city, but east of the main railway line bisecting it. A high curvilinear wall wraps round an asymmetrical auditorium, seating 1,500, and its foyers and restaurants. The wall, which illustrates Aalto's sculptural proclivities, is made of specially designed wedge-shaped bricks.

The Enzo-Gutzeit building (Alvar Aalto, 1962) is the headquarters of a government-controlled wood-pulp and paper corporation. It occupies a prominent position overlooking the South Harbour and is seen as part of the view looking north (page 82) of the early

Helsinki. National Pensions
Institute: the canteen

(*right*)
Helsinki. National Pensions
Institute (1956) by Alvar Aalto

(*far right*)
Helsinki. Palace Hotel (1952) by
Viljo Rewell and Keijo Petäjä

(*below right*)
Helsinki. Meilahti primary
school (1952) by Viljo Rewell and
Osmo Sipari

Helsinki. 'House of Culture'
(1958) by Alvar Aalto

nineteenth-century waterfront buildings with the Lutheran cathedral rising behind them. To conform, it has been designed to present a horizontal mass, white in colour, but the walling material is hard Carrara marble in contrast to the softer-textured stucco predominating in the neoclassical buildings near by. The façades are heavily modelled, the marble surround of each window being shaped into an angular profile.

The Palace Hotel, on the waterfront facing the South Harbour (Viljo Rewell and Keijo Petäjä), is a combined hotel and office building completed in 1952 (following a competition held in 1949) to serve as the headquarters for the Olympic Games. On the ground floor are shops and the entrance foyer of the hotel; from the latter lifts serve the hotel bedrooms on the upper floors and a restaurant on the first floor, the intermediate floors containing offices with separate access. The building, which is faced with slabs of reconstructed stone, owes its somewhat austere character partly to the time of economic stringency at which it was built but also to a positive reaction against the romanticism then still evident in Aalto's and some other architects' work.

The Meilahti primary school (Viljo Rewell and Osmo Sipari, 1952), in a northern residential district of Helsinki, has an undulating two-storey classroom wing with an assembly hall behind. It has a reinforced concrete frame with panel infilling of brick and was the first Finnish school of this type.

Another distinguished school—the secondary school at Kulosaari (Swedish, Brändö), an island suburb to the east of Helsinki, first laid out in 1907 by Lars Sonck, has this assembly hall as its centre, with fixed raking seats, an open timber roof of unusual design and stairs bracketed out from the side wall. These lead to the upper-floor classrooms. The school, built in 1955, is by Jorma Järvi, who was a pioneer of modern Finnish school-building but died in 1962 at the early age of fifty-four. He also designed Helsinki's Olympic swimming-pool, completed in 1952.

The 'Porthania' building of the university (Aarne Ervi, 1957) adjoins the old university area, being sited in Hallituskatu immediately to the west of Engel's library. It houses the faculties of law, mathematics and language and also contains several large auditoria. It was the first building in Helsinki of prestressed, prefabricated reinforced concrete construction, and has some spectacular free-standing staircases. It is faced on the outside with ceramic mosaic.

A school that more closely follows the post-war international idiom is the Finnish-Russian school in an eastern suburb of the city, designed by Osmo Sipari in 1964. It is planned so that each of the three main departments—kindergarten, primary school and secondary school—can operate independently and there is space for a students' hostel. The gymnasium and auditorium (a corner of which can be seen on the right of the photograph) are located so that they can also be used for outside functions. Walls are of prefabricated concrete units.

The City Theatre, by Timo Penttilä (1967) stands surrounded by grass and trees on a sloping site just north of the city centre, overlooking Töölö bay. It has a large auditorium seating 920 and a small one seating 300. Their foyers are grouped so that both have a view of the lake. The building has a reinforced concrete structure with the external walls faced with buff-coloured ceramic tiles.

Helsinki. Secondary school at Kulosaari (1955) by Jorma Järvi: assembly hall

Helsinki. 'Porthania' university building (1957) by Aarne Ervi

Helsinki. Finnish–Russian school
(1964) by Osmo Sipari

Helsinki. The City Theatre (1967)
by Timo Penttilä

Helsinki. Taivallahti church (1969) by Timo and Tuomo Suomalainen

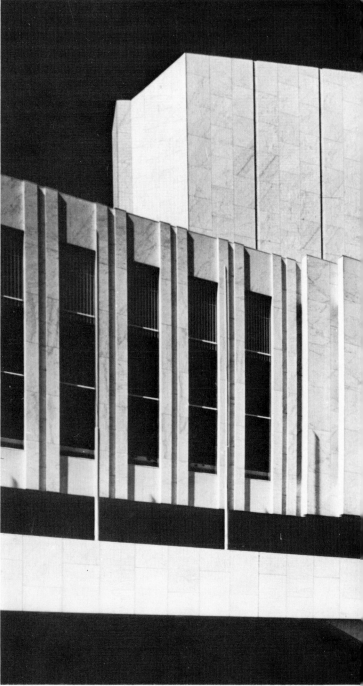

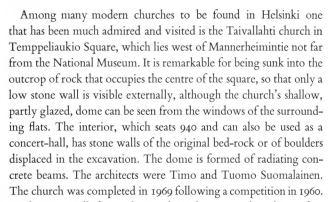

Helsinki City Hall: foyer (1970) by Aarno Ruusuvuori; view looking into the reception hall (1863) by A. H. Dalström

Among many modern churches to be found in Helsinki one that has been much admired and visited is the Taivallahti church in Temppeliaukio Square, which lies west of Mannerheimintie not far from the National Museum. It is remarkable for being sunk into the outcrop of rock that occupies the centre of the square, so that only a low stone wall is visible externally, although the church's shallow, partly glazed, dome can be seen from the windows of the surrounding flats. The interior, which seats 940 and can also be used as a concert-hall, has stone walls of the original bed-rock or of boulders displaced in the excavation. The dome is formed of radiating concrete beams. The architects were Timo and Tuomo Suomalainen. The church was completed in 1969 following a competition in 1960.

The City Hall, facing the South Harbour, was the subject of an extensive renovation programme by Aarno Ruusuvuori in 1970, by means of which modern offices and committee-rooms were created inside the existing Empire-period building designed by C. L. Engel in 1829–33 (see pages 69 and 82) and a parking garage inserted beneath it, while the ceremonial interior spaces were preserved and the exterior restored to its original form. The building had first been a hotel and contained a handsome series of public rooms, including a pillared hall with galleries, added to Engel's building by A. H. Dalström in 1863 and extended by B. A. Granholm in 1887. This hall is retained, and is seen in the photograph through the glazed screen separating it from the new foyer which Ruusuvuori introduced between it and the perimeter offices. This connects with a large new entrance foyer beneath the hall. The strictly functional, but elegantly detailed, offices and circulation spaces admirably set off the florid nineteenth-century interiors.

Helsinki. Finlandia Hall (1971) by Alvar Aalto

Plan of Finlandia Hall at main level

1 large concert hall
2 small (chamber music) hall
3 restaurant
4 foyer
5 private foyer
6 foyer to small hall
7 conference foyer
  (conference halls above)
8 meeting rooms
9 orchestra foyer
10 offices and artists' rooms
11 staff cafeteria
12 kitchen

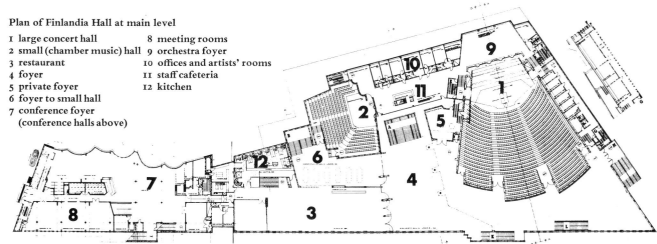

The Finlandia Hall was Alvar Aalto's last important work. It was intended to be the first of a string of public buildings which he had sited along the shore of Töölö bay, just north of the centre of the city, when he made the plan for a new civic centre between 1959 and 1964—a plan now unlikely to proceed further. Finlandia, as first completed in 1971, was simply a concert-hall, albeit a monumentally spacious one; in 1975 Aalto extended it with a wing for conferences, which can be used either independently or in conjunction with the concert-hall's foyers and other subsidiary accommodation. The main concert-hall seats 1,750. There is a small hall for chamber music, seating 350, and a restaurant for 300. The later wing contains two conference rooms which can be combined into one hall seating 900. The whole exterior, with its sharply modelled fly-towers and wall and window surfaces, is faced with white marble.

The Marimekko clothing factory at Herttoniemi, north east of the city, was completed in 1973 and shows the skilful handling of industrial forms and techniques that had been characteristic of Finnish architecture since the pioneer contributions of Lindqvist, Aalto and Huttunen in the 1930s and even earlier. The architects of the factory were Erkki Kairamo and Reijo Lahtinen.

Industrialization has come more recently to housing. A successful instance of the use of standard prefabricated components is the Domino system, here used for an estate of two-storey houses by Esko Kahri and Kai Lohman at Kannelmäki, on the north-eastern edge of Helsinki. They were completed in 1975, and are laid out in short terraces with both communal and private gardens. Completely prefabricated wall-panels have steel frames filled in with wood boarding, the latter painted in a variety of colours—as at Käpylä (pages 140-1), in many ways the prototype of this concept of housing.

Helsinki. Finlandia Hall:
conference wing (1975) by Alvar
Aalto

Helsinki. Marimekko clothing
factory, Herttoniemi (1973) by
Kairamo and Lahtinen

Helsinki. Finlandia Hall: main
foyer

Helsinki. Housing at Kannelmäki (1975) by Kahri and
Lohman

Tapiola. Administrative centre (1961) by Aarne Ervi

Tapiola (Swedish, Hagalund)

This internationally admired satellite town, about 8km (5 miles) west of the centre of Helsinki, was begun in 1952 and in the early 1970s reached its planned final population of 18,000. The town was founded by a number of welfare and housing organizations who jointly established the Asuntosäätiö building society, a non profit-making organization, to plan and finance it. It consists of three residential neighbourhoods of approximately equal size, each with a mixture of terrace houses and tall flats built to an overall density of 120 people per hectare (2.5 acres), set among trees and winding roads. They are grouped round an administrative and shopping centre which was the subject of a competition in 1954, won by

Aarne Ervi. The centre includes the tower block, containing offices and a top floor restaurant, and the shopping square illustrated (both 1961) and is sited alongside a large open space containing a lake, with a secondary school nearby. This space is now (1977) being partly filled by further community buildings, which will give the centre of the town a coherence it previously lacked. Another late development has been to introduce a small amount of industry and offices to provide more local employment and prevent Tapiola from being wholly a satellite town for commuters to Helsinki. All the dwellings in Tapiola are supplied with heating, hot water and electricity from one central power station.

Tapiola. Shopping centre (1961)
by Aarne Ervi

Tapiola. Studio houses (1956) by
Aulis Blomstedt

Tapiola. Flats (1958) by Viljo Rewell

Tapiola. Houses (1959) by Kaija and Heikki Siren

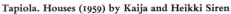

Tapiola. Suvikumpu housing (1967–9) by Reima Pietilä

The houses and flats have been designed by a number of architects. The standard both of architecture and of landscaping is, with very few exceptions, high. Four typical examples are illustrated here: a terrace of studio houses (Aulis Blomstedt, 1956), each with a double-height studio with a gallery across one end; a four-storey block of flats (Viljo Rewell, 1958) surrounding a green quadrangle; one of a row of fairly luxurious separate houses (Kaija and Heikki Siren, 1959), making use of a sloping site to raise the main floor well above road level, at which level there is a double garage with the living-room extending over it and terminating in a south-facing balcony; and the Suvikumpu housing, consisting of four blocks of varying height (see plan), each containing 140 flats, with a block of shops and garages in the centre. This last housing project was the outcome of a competition, won in 1962 by Reima Pietilä and Raili Paatelainen. It was built in 1967–9. The walls are of concrete and wood boarding, the latter, and the ribbed concrete balconies, being painted green.

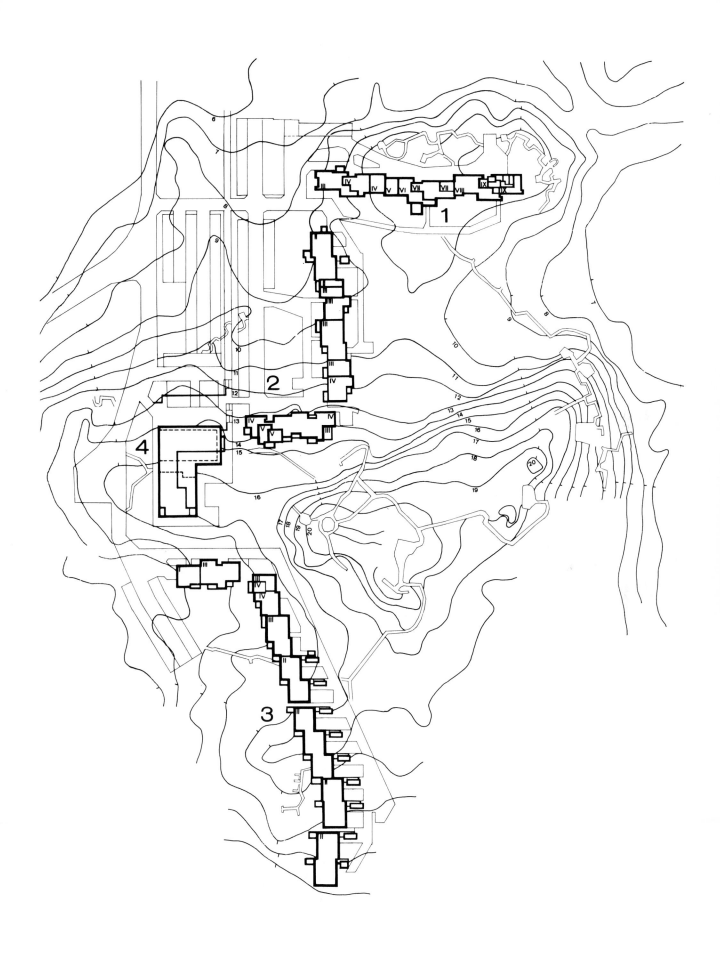

Layout plan of Suvikumpu housing, Tapiola

Otaniemi. Institute of Technology main building (1964) by Alvar Aalto

Otaniemi

On this peninsula, north east of Tapiola, are sited the Helsinki Institute of Technology and the State Institute of Technical Research. It is laid out according to a plan made by Alvar Aalto in 1949, and a number of the buildings are also by him. These include the main Institute of Technology building, designed in 1964 and marking a return to his earlier, more expressionist, style. It houses several faculties, the central administration and auditoria, the largest auditorium being contained in the tall block, curved in plan and triangular in section, seen in the photograph. The foyers open onto raised terraces partly enclosed by the wings of the building.

The several blocks of student living accommodation (Heikki Siren and M. Melakari), a sports hall (Aalto), used for the 1952 Olympic Games, and a students' restaurant (Kaija and Heikki Siren),

were all built in 1952. The interior of the restaurant, illustrated here, is typically expressive and vigorous in its use of wood construction. The material is used scientifically, yet with the live muscular quality more often found in the work of unselfconscious craftsmen, such as boat-builders. Also at Otaniemi is an elaborately romantic students' union building known as Dipoli, by Reima Pietilä (1966), and until recently there was a modest, but unusually beautiful, students' chapel built by Kaija and Heikki Siren in 1957, but this was destroyed by fire in 1975. It will however be rebuilt.

Otaniemi. Students' restaurant (1952) by Kaija and Heikki Siren

Turku. The Sibelius Museum
(1968) by Woldemar Baeckman

Turku. Marina Palace Hotel (1974)
by Jaakko and Unto Rantanen

Tampere University (1962) by T. Korhonen and J. Laapotti: the main wing

Turku (Swedish, Åbo)

In the university area surrounding the cathedral (seen in the background of the photograph and described on pages 25-6) is the Sibelius Museum by Woldemar Baeckman (1968). It is a single-storey concrete building containing beautifully arranged exhibition galleries surrounding a clerestory-lit recital hall.

The Marina Palace Hotel, by Jaakko and Unto Rantanen, is Turku's newest luxury hotel, completed in 1974. It occupies a site on the riverbank, opposite the municipal theatre, where nineteenth-century houses are being replaced by modern buildings. The hotel has three floors of bedrooms projecting over a high ground floor containing public rooms, restaurants etc, and another restaurant with a roof-terrace on the top floor. It is faced with light-coloured ceramic tiles.

Tampere (Swedish, Tammerfors)

The main building of the university was built in 1962 by Toivo Korhonen and Jaakko Laapotti. It is cruciform in shape, with lecture halls in the centre of the main wing and other rooms that need high ceilings, such as refectories and libraries, at either end of it. Teaching, study and administrative rooms occupy the transverse wing, on two floors. The building has (unusually in Finland) a steel frame and pre-cast wall panels with a marble aggregate. The roof of the main lecture hall is suspended from beams exposed on the outside of the building. These can be seen in the photograph, which shows the west façade and the windows of the refectory.

Tampere. Kaleva church (1966)
by Reima Pietilä

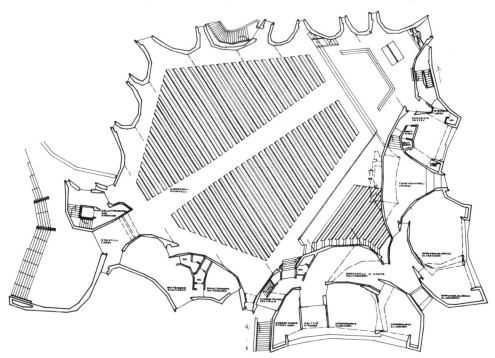

Plan of Kaleva church,
Tampere

About 13km (eight miles) from Tampere is the Vatiala cemetery with a reinforced concrete chapel (1962) by Viljo Rewell in a well landscaped setting of lawns and trees. The building, the subject of a competition, contains a large and a small chapel separated by a hall. The large chapel has a parabolic roof covered with copper. This is only one of a number of interestingly designed funeral chapels recently built in Finland. Others are at Turku, (by Pekka Pitkänen), at Vaasa (by Juhani Katainen), at Hamina (by Tino and Tuomo Suomalainen) and at Oulu (by Seppo Valjus).

On the edge of the city stands the most ambitious new church in Finland: the Kaleva Church, by Reima Pietilä, the outcome of a competition held in 1959. The church, which stands on high ground dominating a residential area, was completed in 1966. It holds 1,050 and has a gallery for a choir of eighty. The intention was to line the interior walls with acoustic tiles and leave the structural concrete exposed externally. In fact the reverse has been done: the contrete is left exposed inside and the outside of the building is faced with ceramic tiles.

Tampere. Kaleva church: interior

Tampere. Vatiala cemetery chapel (1962) by Viljo Rewell

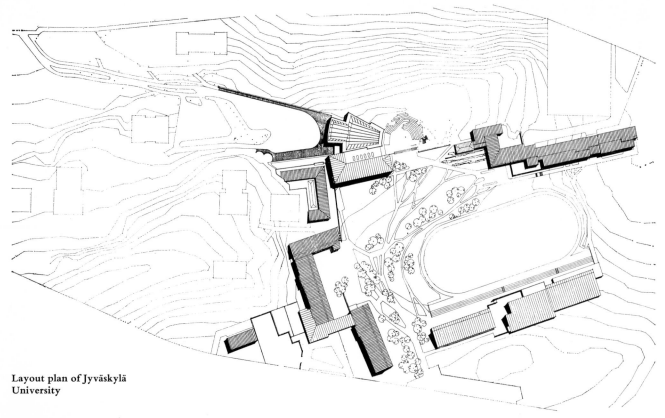

Layout plan of Jyväskylä
University

Jyväskylä University: staircase
hall in main building

Jyväskylä

This town in mid-Finland has a long educational tradition, having been the first place to institute teaching in the Finnish language in 1858. Here the central teachers' training college for the whole of Finland was founded in 1863. Its nineteenth-century buildings, now providing students' living accommodation, were supplemented by a range of new buildings by Alvar Aalto in 1950, and the whole group is now the university.

Aalto's buildings, mostly in his favourite hard red brick, are arranged round three sides of a long narrow sports field (right of plan on page 176). On the east are the staff refectory (shown in close-up in the photograph), the students' refectory and a dormitory; on the north the library; on the west a gymnasium and a swimming-bath. At the north-east corner is the main teaching building with a large entrance foyer on the axis of the road by which the college is approached through its wooded grounds—the road being an extension of the main street of the town. This foyer, which leads to a large auditorium, has on its left a glass wall dramatically revealing the forest scenery outside and on its right the long staircase hall illustrated, which serves smaller auditoria, laboratories and studios. This hall exemplifies Aalto's skilful and imaginative handling of interior space.

Also by Aalto, and close to the grounds of the training college, is the Central Finnish Museum (1961), a modest white-walled building overlooking a steep grassy bank. In Jyväskylä, too, can be seen a number of Aalto's early works, designed in neoclassical style before he moved to Turku in 1927. (see page 142)

Rovaniemi. Bus terminus (1959)
by Pulkka, Rajala and Leppänen

Rovaniemi. Library (1965) by
Alvar Aalto

Rovaniemi

Close to the Arctic Circle, Rovaniemi is the administrative capital of Finnish Lapland. The town was almost totally destroyed by German troops in 1944. Rebuilding followed a plan drawn up by Alvar Aalto. It is an important communications centre, especially for long-distance bus routes, and has a bus terminus incorporating a small hotel and restaurant, by Niilo Pulkka, Pekka Rajala and Kaarlo Leppänen, completed in 1959 (competition 1956). The windows are triple-glazed to protect the interior against the extreme cold. The sculpturally shaped upper walls are faced with wood boarding.

The municipal library is one of a group of three buildings designed by Alvar Aalto to form a civic and cultural centre for Rovaniemi. A conference hall has also been completed but the town offices are not yet begun. The library, shown here, was built in 1965 and has one of Aalto's most successful late interiors with several changes of level and with lighting designed to exploit the low northern sun. It includes an exhibition room and small auditorium and, in the basement, a music library and museum. The exterior is faced with ribbed ceramic tiles.

**Rovaniemi. Ounasvaara Hotel
(1968) by Jaakko Laapotti**

**Section through
Ounasvaara Hotel**

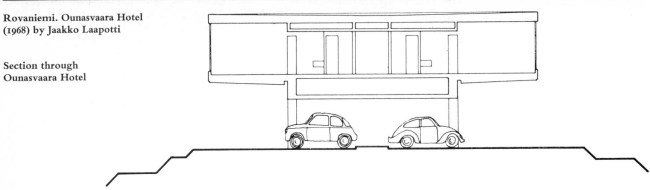

The Ounasvaara Hotel, primarily for winter sports, is just outside Rovaniemi and was designed by Jaakko Laapotti in 1968. It occupies the crown of a rocky hill and has carparking at the lower level, together with the reception; all other accommodation is raised to the upper floor so as to make the most of the view. There are thirty-nine bedrooms and a restaurant seating 200. The frame is reinforced concrete faced with wood.

Oulu (Swedish, Uleåborg)

This thriving industrial and seaport town has ambitious plans for a civic centre of which only the first building has been completed: a theatre, by Marjatta and Martti Jaatinen, on the water's edge near the old harbour. It was built in 1972 and will be followed by a library and town offices by the same architects. These will occupy the level space on the right of the photograph. The theatre is a crisply detailed steel and glass building in a severely Miesian style.

Oulu has also a new university campus at Linnanmaa, a little way north of the town, which is being built in stages to supplement the original university, founded in 1958 at Kontinkangas, to the south east. This will eventually house only the medical faculties, all the others being concentrated in the new buildings at Linnanmaa. These, designed by Kari Virta from 1969 onwards, are on two main levels enclosing a series of courtyards and allowing communication between all departments, and between teaching rooms, lecture halls and social accommodation, under cover. On the outside of the buildings, pale neutral colours are enlivened by patches of brilliant colour, and inside strong colour is used for identification as well as decorative purposes.

Oulu. Civic Theatre (1972) by
Marjatta and Martti Jaatinen

Oulu University buildings,
Linnanmaa (1969) by Kari Virta

Kouvola

This growing industrial town—also an important railway junction —east of Helsinki, has one of the best of a number of recently built town-halls, combining the functions of civic centre and town offices. Designed by Bertel Saarnio and Juha Leiviskä, who won a competition held in 1964, it was completed in 1969. It is partly raised on pillars to give access to an internal court from which the public rooms are reached and which separates them from the offices. The photograph, looking into this court, shows the disciplined use of industrially made materials typical of the best work by the younger generation of Finnish architects.

Seinäjoki

In 1952 Alvar Aalto won the competition for a church in the proposed civic centre on the edge of this growing industrial town in the flat Ostrobothnian plain, south east of Vaasa. It was completed in

Seinäjoki town hall (1964) by
Alvar Aalto

1960, and, while it was being built, Aalto won another competition
for the civic centre itself, separated from the church by a main road.
Two of the buildings, a town hall and a library, were completed in
1964. A theatre and a range of parish offices are to follow, the latter
forming a square with the west end of the church. The photograph
shows one end of the town-hall which has walls faced with Aalto's
favourite rounded tiles (see under the National Pensions Institute,
Helsinki, pages 158-9) in dark blue, highly glazed. The main floor is
on an upper level and the staircase hall at street level is approached
through a colonnade beneath it. Rising through the main floor is the
triangular upper part of the council chamber. From the pedestrian
square at the other side of the building—between it and the library—
the upper level can be reached directly by climbing a stepped, grass-
grown slope, and from there another outside stair, in a slit between
two tile-faced walls, leads still higher to the council chamber's
public gallery.

**Vuoksenniska church (1959) by
Alvar Aalto**

Vuoksenniska

In a loosely scattered industrial area surrounding the town of Imatra (see pages 132-3), in south-eastern Finland, right on the Russian frontier, is this church by Alvar Aalto, completed in 1959. It is sited among trees, and the tower has been given a distinctive outline so that it can be easily identified among the many factory chimneys which also rise above the trees and with which it cannot compete in height. Vuoksenniska Church, which has white plastered walls and copper roofs, has an ingeniously complex plan-shape, based on the need to enlarge or reduce its seating capacity at will and to enable it to serve various purposes. There are three areas, each with one straight and one rounded side wall, separated by sliding partitions. The first, containing also the altar and pulpit, can serve as a chapel for wedding and funeral services and the like. By opening the partitions, space can be made for successively larger congregations, and the two outer areas can be used separately, with the partitions closed, for social purposes.

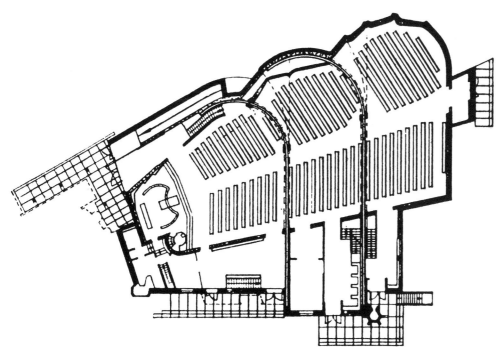

Plan of Vuoksenniska church

Vuoksenniska church; interior

Hyvinkää church (1961) by Aarno Ruusuvuori

Hyvinkää

On rocky tree-planted ground near the centre of this rapidly grow-ing town, 45km (28 miles) north of Helsinki, stands this church of unusual triangular outline. It was designed by Aarno Ruusuvuori in 1961, following a competition. It seats 630 with another sixty in the organ and choir-loft. There is also a parish hall seating 200 which is placed above the entrance vestibule and can be opened into the upper part of the church to serve as a gallery. The building has a rhomboidal plan divided from corner to corner, so that the church itself, occupying half the area, is triangular in plan. It is also tri-angular in section, rising to a peak in the centre of the building. The other half is also triangular in section but not so high, allowing clerestory lighting into the church above the gallery. The building is of reinforced concrete with the long sloping ribs filled in with glass or precast concrete slabs.

Kaskinen

This is in a village south of Vaasa. The church was designed by Erik Kråkström and completed in 1965. It stands on rocky ground surrounded by tall trees and seats 2,000. It has a parish hall and club-room alongside. Construction is brick and timber, the latter stained dark brown.

The three churches illustrated above were among the earliest of an impressive series of modern churches built in Finland in the 1960s and 1970s, nearly all the outcome of competitions. Others out-standing are at Lauttasaari, Helsinki (by Keijo Petäjä, 1958), at Huutoniemi, near Vaasa (by Aarno Ruusuvuori, 1964), in the Herttoniemi district of Helsinki (by Lauri Silvennoinen, 1970) and at Oulu (by Juha Leiviskä, 1976).

Kaskinen church (1965) by Erik Kräkström

Bibliography

The following is a short list of books on Finnish architecture written wholly in English or with some of the text or captions translated into English.

Ahmavaara, Anna-Liisa. *Living Close to Nature* (Helsinki: Otava, 1966) Photographs, plans and brief notes on 24 modern private houses with a rural or suburban setting. The very short introduction and a note on each house are in English.

Ålander, Kyösti (ed). *Viljo Rewell: works and projects* (Helsinki: Otava, 1966) Largely pictorial survey of the work of this leading and influential architect, who died too young in 1964, by the late director of the Museum of Finnish Architecture. Text in English and German.

Art Treasures of Medieval Finland (Helsinki: Otava. No date) Picture book (photographs by István Rácz) chiefly concerned with wall-paintings and sculpture but with notes at the end on the churches in which they are found. These are in English; so is the short introduction. Captions to the pictures in Finnish only.

Boulton Smith, John. *The Golden Age of Finnish Art* (Helsinki: Otava, 1976) A short but knowledgeable account of the arts in Finland at the beginning of this century, with proper weight given to the part played by architecture. In English.

Christ-Janer, Albert. *Eliel Saarinen* (University of Chicago Press, 1948) Illustrated biography.

Finland's Most Beautiful Churches (Jyväskylä: K. J. Gummerus, 1962) Picture book with introduction (by Antero Sinisalo) and captions in Finnish, Swedish, English and German. Architectural notes at the end in Finnish only.

Fleig, Karl (ed). *Alvar Aalto* (Zurich: Girsberger, 1963 and 1971) The architect's complete works until 1970 illustrated and described in two volumes. Text in German, English and French.

Gutheim, Frederick. *Alvar Aalto*, Masters of World Architecture series (New York: George Braziller; London: Mayflower, 1960) General account of Aalto's career up to the late 1950s.

Helsinki Architectural Guide (Otava, 1976) Invaluable pocket guide to old and modern buildings, compiled by the Finnish Architectural Museum. Introduction (by Otto I Meurman); some photographs; notes on the buildings in Finnish, Swedish and English.

Hertzen, H. von, and Spreiregen, P. D. *Building a New Town: Finland's new garden city, Tapiola* (Cambridge, Mass and London: MIT Press, 1971) More useful for facts and figures about Tapiola than as an architectural assessment.

Neuenschwander, E. and C. *Alvar Aalto and Finnish Architecture* (London: Architectural Press, 1954) Text in German, English and French.

Salokorpi, Asko. *Modern Architecture in Finland* (London, Weidenfeld and Nicolson, 1970) A small but well chosen pictorial anthology, with a good introduction and a very brief note about each building shown. In English only.

Siren (Helsinki: Otava, 1977) Picture-book on the work of the contemporary architects Kaija and Heikki Siren. Minimum text (in English and German). Introduction by Jürgen Joedicke. In English, French and German.

Suolahti, Eino E. *Helsinki: a City in a Classic Style* (Helsinki: Otava, 1973) Brief but scholarly account of the rebuilding of Helsinki between 1812 and 1852. In English. Good colour photographs but lacks a plan.

Wickberg, Nils Erik. *Finnish Architecture* (Helsinki: Otava, 1959) Picture book with short text. The best general account by a Finnish historian. In English.

Wickberg, Nils Erik. *Carl Ludwig Engel* (Helsinki: Otava, 1970). In English.

The best traveller's guide-books in English are the *Finland* volume in the Nagel Travel Guide series (Geneva, latest edition 1971), and *The Travellers' Guide to Finland*, by Sylvie Nickels (Jonathan Cape, London, 1965).

Photographic acknowledgements

Copyright Owners and Photographers

J. M. Richards: 15, 16, 19, 20, 21, 25, 32 (top left and right, bottom left), 33, 34, 35, 36, 37, 40, 42, 45 (top), 46 (top), 47 (bottom), 48, 50 (top), 51, 52, 53, 59, 60 (top), 61 (top), 64, 66 (bottom), 67, 70, 71, 73, 74, 75 (bottom), 76, 77, 79, 80 (top), 83 (bottom), 84, 85, 86, 87, 88 (bottom), 89, 90 (bottom), 91, 92 (top), 96, 97, 98, 99, 100, 101, 102, 103, 104, 105, 106, 110, 111, 112, 113, 114 (bottom), 115, 118, 121, 126 (bottom), 129, 130, 131 (bottom), 132, 133, 134, 135, 136, 137, 144, 145, 149, 155, 157 (bottom), 162 (top), 166, 167, 168 (top), 172 (bottom), 173, 174, 175 (bottom), 177, 178 (bottom), 181, 183, 184, 186.

Museum of Finnish Architecture, Helsinki: 11, 13 (top) A. Salokorpi, 14 Helamaa, 17 N. E. Wickberg, 22, 23 Rista, 24 (bottom) István Rácz, 43 P. Laurila, 44 Kari Hakli, 50 (bottom) A. Salokorpi, 54, 55 Kari Hakli, 60 (bottom) N. E. Wickberg, 61 Helamaa, 62-3 Oy Sääski, 65 (bottom) N. E. Wickberg, 72 Air Forces, 78 Karhumäki, 81 A. Salokorpi, 83 (top) Museum of Finnish Architecture, 88 (top) F. Runeberg, 90 (top), 92 (bottom) A. Salokorpi, 93 Iffland, 95 A. Salokorpi, 107 Havas, 109 (top) A. Ruusuvuori, 109 (bottom) István Rácz, 114 (top) A. Salokorpi, 119 Loja Saarinen, 120 Roos, 122 (bottom) N. Wasastjerna, 122 (top), 123 Havas, 124 A. Salokorpi, 125 (top) N. Wasastjerna, 125 (bottom) Havas, 127 Roos, 139 N. Wasastjerna, 140 (bottom) A. Salokorpi, 140-1 Havas, 143 Museum of Finnish Architecture, 146 (top) Apollo, 146 (bottom), 147 (top left) Roos, 147 (bottom) Iffland, 148 Foto Roos, 150 G. Welin, 151 Ov. Foto Ab., 154 Valokuva Oy Kolmio, 158 Havas, 161 (top) Rista, 161 (bottom) M. I. Jaatinen, 162 (bottom) R. Kamunen, 163, 164 Kari Hakli, 165 Rista, 168 (bottom) R. Paatelainen, 170 Ingervo, 172 (top) Rista, 175 (top) Pietilä, 176 Ingervo, 178 (top) Havas, 179, 180 Rista, 182-3 Igor Herler.

K. J. Gummerus, Jyväskylä (G. Welin): 24 (top), 26 (top), 27 (top), 28 (right), 32 (bottom right), 45 (bottom), 47 (top), 56, 57; **National Museum of Finland:** 65 (top), 66 (top); **Turku City Museum:** 75 (top); **Hämeenlinna Museum:** 15 (bottom); **Albin Aaltonen:** 46 (bottom); **Aarne Ervi:** 160; **Havas:** 147 (top right), 156, 157 (top), 159, 167 (bottom), 171; **E. Krakström:** 186; **Roos:** 148; **G. Welin:** 41, 126 (top), 131 (top), 185.

Drawings

Eleven of the plans and other drawings are from originals supplied by the Museum of Finnish Architecture, Helsinki. For permission to reproduce the remainder, thanks are due to the Otava Publishing Co, Helsinki; to Nordisk Rotogravyr, Stockholm; to the Architectural Press, London, and to the architects of the buildings they illustrate.

Index